Dr. Price's

Golden Nuggets

Dr. Price's Golden Nuggets

A Treasury of Wisdom for
Both Ministers and Laypeople

By
Frederick K.C. Price, Ph.D.

Faith One Publishing
Los Angeles, California

Dr. Price's Golden Nuggets
ISBN 1-883798-23-X
Copyright © 1998 by
Frederick K.C. Price, Ph.D.
P.O. Box 90000
Los Angeles, CA 90009

Published by Faith One Publishing
7901 South Vermont Avenue
Los Angeles, California 90044

Contents

Introduction

Throughout his years of ministry, Dr. Frederick K.C. Price has been used by God to bring forth practical insight and biblical issues deeply embedded in the Word of God. These nuggets of biblical wisdom shed brilliant facets of light, enabling people to see the Bible not only as a holy Book, but a Book that is relevant to their everyday lives. As a result of such incisive teaching, Dr. Price has impacted the lives of millions of people, bringing them into a place of knowledge, understanding and victory.

Presented in this book, *Dr. Price's Golden Nuggets,* is a mother lode of truth from a vast mine of messages he has taught. These messages have been requested over and over by those people who faithfully support and follow his ministry. They are thought-provoking lessons on a variety of subjects, including faith — a subject that has earned Fred Price a reputation for being part of the "Name It and Claim It Bunch." These teachings go to the heart of the matter on subjects pertaining to the family, marriage, divorce, prosperity, ministry, improper eating habits, and more.

No matter what he is discussing, Dr. Price's message is delivered in a unique, bold style that always drives the point home for the reader.

Ministers and laypersons alike will want this compendium in their collections. It is one they will turn to and reflect upon repeatedly.

— The Editors

Nugget No. 1

It's Time to Grow Up!

(Excerpted from a message
delivered at an International Charismatic
Bible Ministries Conference)

I want you to know that I love you very much. I love you so much that I will risk you not loving me to give you the truth, the whole truth and nothing but the truth, so help me God. I mean you no harm, but only good.

I want to bring some good news to some of you who apparently are in some struggling-type of situations.

I am thoroughly convinced that our God is a God of principles. And there is a principle in the Kingdom of God by which all things in His Kingdom operate. That principle is faith.

I have been teaching on this subject for more than 25 years, but I believe God has given me brand-new revelation concerning faith and its operation. I always knew that faith is an action, but now I am more sure than ever about that fact.

We say we believe the Word, so we ought to be willing to act on it. Bible faith is acting on the Word of God. If we were acting on the Word, we wouldn't be crying, because there would be nothing to cry about. Yes, there is pain. Yes, there is hurt. Yes, there is sickness. Yes, there are deprivations in life. But do not capitalize on those things. Capitalize on what God says about them. He says you are an overcomer (1 John 4:4). He says you are above and not beneath (Deuteronomy 28:13). He says you are the head and not the tail (Deuteronomy 28:13). You are blessed going out and blessed coming in (Deuteronomy 28:6). Begin to confess those things!

Romans 10:8:

> **But what does it say? "The word is near you, in your mouth and in your heart" (that is, the word of faith which we preach).**

We need to understand that we should come to these conferences to receive, but we need to move out of the babyhood stage. I don't mean this in a condemnatory way. I am simply trying to elevate your sights. I know some people like the crying and complaining, because it is easier to cry and complain than it is to walk by faith. When you walk by faith, it can be scary if you are easily frightened because there is nothing tangible that you can reach out and touch.

I travel all over the world, and everywhere I travel, I hear the same kind of crying, whining and complaining. We all have problems in the sense of being shot at — we're in the same world, and we have the same enemy. The demons do not like you, or me, any less. But we are not going to defeat them by crying and complaining about what they are doing in our lives. Why don't we talk about how big God is? Why not talk about that rather than all the problems and apparent mountains?

So you have a mountain? Big deal! Instead of crying about it, speak to that mountain and get it out of your way! That is what Jesus told us to do.

I have good news for you. You can live above the circumstances if you want to. I realize that for some of you, if you do not have problems, you do not have anything to talk about, because you do not know the Word. So, you have to whine and cry and complain.

You cannot look at the circumstances and be successful in the Kingdom of God. When I say successful, I mean walk in liberty and peace. You can still get work done by struggling and crying and complaining, but it is a whole lot better to get the work done without the struggle, without the crying and without the complaining. I have had many opportunities for "down days," but I retired from down days more than 25 years ago, and I haven't had a "down day" since.

If you want someone to cry with you, I am not the one. If you want somebody to pat you on the back, or pat you on the head and say, "Keep holding on," I'm here to tell you that is not going to help you. You need to know that you can walk by the Word. You can walk by faith. We are not representing Jesus the way we should when we sniffle, cry and complain.

Put On Your Armor!

Because we are in a war, you are being shot at just like me and everybody else in the Body of Christ. What do you expect the enemy to do, but shoot at you? You have armor — put it on!

You have armor — use it! If you have it packed in a trunk in the closet, get it out and put it to use! Why are you crying and whining? Get up on your feet and stand tall, like the child of God that you are! If you are not a winner, don't ever tell anybody that you know Jesus. And certainly don't tell them that you are filled with the Holy Spirit!

You have nerve talking about how hard it is! Big deal! You don't know how hard it is until you know what it is to be Black in America!

Jesus never said, "According to your tears let it be to you." He said, **"According to your faith let it be to you"** (Matthew 9:29).

Several years ago, our congregation bought the Pepperdine University campus, in the ghetto — 32 acres right in the heart of the city. The City of Los Angeles couldn't even buy it. The reason they couldn't was that the property was set aside for Crenshaw Christian Center, because we had learned to walk by faith and not by sight! God honors faith. He will pass over 27,000 people to get to somebody who will dare to believe Him.

We had every demon and all of their cousins, aunts, uncles — even their dogs and frogs — in the Western Hemisphere come against us when we were building our FaithDome sanctuary. I never knew there were so many demons. They came against us to try to stop the Word of God. But I never confessed that we were sinking.

On the day that our FaithDome sanctuary was dedicated, the facility was fully paid for — $26,000,000 — by Black folk in the ghetto! Now you absolutely, positively, unequivocally know that if God would do that for a Black man in the ghetto, you can imagine what He will do for you with white skin in the suburbs!

I want to encourage and inspire you. You can live above the circumstances!

Matthew 8:23-25:

> **Now when He got into a boat, His disciples followed Him.**
> **And suddenly a great tempest arose on the sea, so that the boat was covered with the waves. But He was asleep.**
> **Then His disciples came to Him and awoke Him, saying, "Lord, save us! We are perishing!"**

The boat was still afloat and the disciples were already confessing they were perishing. That is what some of us have been doing — confessing defeat instead of victory. Every time you whine, complain, and cry, you are giving the devil comfort; you are not honoring God. If you just have to say something, say, "Praise the Lord, glory to God, hallelujah." And if your mouth wants to say anything else, slap yourself!

Matthew 8:26:

> **But He said to them, "Why are you fearful, O you of little faith?" Then He arose and rebuked the winds and the sea, and there was a great calm.**

He did not say they didn't have any faith. He said they had "little." But you can perish with a little faith if you don't "put some feet" to what you believe by acting on it.

Jesus didn't just lie on His pillow and say, "Well, I believe the storm will stop. Jehovah will do something about the storm."

The Bible says He got up from His nap. He arose and rebuked. Those are actions. It is not thinking or believing something that will change a particular situation. It is doing something. That is why Jesus called their faith "little" — because their faith did nothing. They had it, but they did not use it. Instead of saying, "Be still," they said, "We are perishing."

Jesus had to believe that when He arose and rebuked, the winds and the sea would obey. So, you start out with belief, but if you stay with only the belief, you are going to sink. Belief won't change the circumstances, but faith will.

The devil has no right to put something on you that will destroy you. But we are in a warfare, and we will be shot at. My wife and I stood and confessed the Word for two years when she was going through a physical challenge. Today she is completely whole. The Bible says, **No temptation has overtaken you except such as is common to man; but God is faithful, who will not allow you to be tempted beyond what you are able, but with the temptation will also make the way of escape, that you may be able to bear it** (1 Corinthians 10:13).

So it could not be God bringing the problem, because if that were so, He would be working against Himself. The devil is the culprit, and God is the Deliverer!

Faith — The Most Important Subject

The most important subject in the Bible, in the Kingdom of God, once you receive Christ as your Savior and Lord, is the subject of faith. It is the most important thing for you to understand and master, once you are saved. There is no other subject more important, and I will challenge anyone to prove otherwise.

Some people might say that love is more important, according to 1 Corinthians 13:13. But love is not the greatest thing in the world. In that chapter, Paul is talking about love as our motivation, while chapters 12 and 14 deal with the power of the Holy Spirit, and why we should desire spiritual gifts.

I believe in love, but love will not heal you. Love will not save you. Love will not pay your bills. You should operate in love, because the love of God has been poured out in our hearts by the Holy Spirit. But probably every single one of us could attest to the fact that we have stood beside the bed of somebody we loved with all of our hearts. We watched that person, our hearts breaking and tears in our eyes. Our whole visage was changed because of that individual we loved lying on that bed. Yet, our love could not keep them alive. If it could, we would never have had the funeral.

Because I am sold on faith, I am very zealous about it. That is why I come off so strong. Sometimes I need to say things to get your attention, and people get upset with me.

Once in a while, I get on people who are overweight. I don't like that job, but somebody has to challenge them. Somebody has to speak the truth instead of lying to them, saying, "You look good full-figured." I tell them it is not healthy. If you are overweight, the extra pounds are working a hardship on your organs. How could you be spiritually in tune and be out of control physically? You can see your physical body. You wash it. You bathe it. You deodorize it, you brush your teeth and you clothe it.

You can see it and it is out of control. How are you going to do anything with your spirit and you can't even see it?

I talk about the songs people are used to hearing in church — songs that are so unscriptural. Faith comes by hearing. So, if I keep on singing something that is unscriptural, it is going to affect my faith in a negative way.

"Cumbiya. Come by here, Lord. Somebody needs you, Lord, come by here." It's a beautiful song. But I thought the Man told you, **"For where two or three are gathered together in My name, I am there in the midst of them"** (Matthew 18:20). So, what's the matter with you? Do you think the Man's lying to you?

The Bible says, **pray without ceasing** (1 Thessalonians 5:17). That is a command of God, so whether I feel like it or not, I do it by faith, not by feelings. Yet there is a song that says, "Every time I feel the Spirit moving in my heart, I will pray." We do everything in this world by our senses, and people unwittingly bring that same *modus operandi* into the realm of the spirit. They want to see God, and feel God.

Then there is another song which says, "Jesus, keep me near the cross, there's a precious fountain." Why do you want to stay near the cross? The cross is a place of death! If you want to sing something like that, sing, "Keep me near the empty tomb ..." because the resurrection is a sign of victory. You start at the cross, but you don't end at the cross. You end at the empty tomb and at the Throne of God!

I hear people talk about being "slain in the Spirit." This statement gives the impression that somebody died in the Spirit. God is not killing us! Show me any verse in the New Testament that mentions "slain in the Spirit." I'm a stickler for the New

Covenant, and you do not find anything in there that says "slain in the Spirit." You do not find anything in the New Covenant that says we are going to win any victories by praise either. Sometimes, our words get us into trouble. Why don't we just say what the Word says!

We are not under the Old Covenant. We are under the New Covenant — a better covenant, which was established on better promises (Hebrews 8:6). That is why when I hear something that is unscriptural, something that is not New Testament, I feel an obligation by the Spirit of God to deal with it.

Under the Old Covenant, people were anointed. They were not filled with the Spirit like we are under the New Covenant. They had to have an anointing. You do not find anything about a double anointing in the New Testament, such as Elisha had in the Old Covenant.

How can you have double of that which is perfect? The scripture says, **... He who is in you is greater than he who is in the world** (1 John 4:4). This scripture does not say you need to have the anointing come on you. It says to be *filled* with the Spirit.

The Holy Spirit is the anointing in us. He works through us, not on us, as He did in the Old Covenant. Everyone in the Old Covenant — including Elisha — was a sinner. They were spiritually dead and had no contact with God. Therefore, He had to deal with them outwardly, in the realm of the senses. That is why He had to put a pillar of cloud by day and pillar of fire by night for them to be guided by. But there is no mention of pillars in the New Covenant. It says, **For we walk by faith, not by sight** (2 Corinthians 5:7).

9

When God gave you the first anointing, it was enough! Walk in it! But you are going to have to do it by faith. If you are waiting to see something — to walk by sight — it's too late. You have to walk by faith, which means you have to walk by the Word!

In the Book of Ephesians, when Jesus went back to heaven and led captivity captive, it says He gave gifts to men — apostles, prophets, evangelists, pastors, and teachers. Why did God give us those gifts? The King James Bible says it was for the perfecting of the saints. In other words, it was for the maturing of the saints — the growing up of the saints. God wants us to grow up and not be babies.

Crying is a baby tendency. Adults don't cry like babies, not in the same sense. You expect babies to cry. But some of us have been on the road for 99 years and we're still crying! That is immaturity. The ministry gifts are not working too well for these carnal Christians, because they should be growing up.

I want to help stimulate you to grow up. I want you to learn to stand on your own faith feet, and not have to rely on anyone, because people can let you down. They do not mean to, but they can fall, and what will you do then? When some well-known ministers fell, people were saying, "What are we going to do now?" Well, your faith should have been in Jesus, not in those men! I am sorry those men fell. It hurt me deeply. But the Book says, **looking unto Jesus, the author and finisher of our faith** (Hebrews 12:2).

I was grieved when these brothers had challenges and succumbed to them. But we have to grow up!

What is especially tragic to me is how people think you are on somebody's case when you speak the truth boldly. We must start working together, and maybe the people outside the Body of Christ will really believe we know God when we stop throwing rocks at each other just because we don't understand the other person's mission. And we need to accept the truth when it is told.

I consider myself a man of principle, and if I have to make a choice between friendship and a principle, then I have to go with principle. I am going to be obedient to what God has called me to do, which is to teach His Word, to tell you the truth — without compromise.

And the truth, the whole truth, and nothing but the truth is that whining, crying, judging, bellyaching and complaining have never moved mountains. But faith has and always will!

Nugget No. 2

How to be Bold in the Lord

I believe the Church today can learn some marvelous lessons from Acts 4:29-30:

> **"Now, Lord, look on their threats, and grant to Your servants that with all boldness they may speak Your word,**
> **"by stretching out Your hand to heal, and that signs and wonders may be done through the name of Your holy Servant Jesus."**

The people were saying that if God would stretch forth His hand to heal and do signs and wonders, they would be bold. I wonder if that is why so many Christians, churches, and ministers of the Gospel are not very bold in proclaiming the name of Jesus. Because they have not seen signs, wonders and healings take place in their churches or in their lives, the people in these congregations have not been very bold to proclaim the Gospel of Christ.

These people are like the ones who prayed in Acts. They have the attitude that once God manifests something supernaturally in their midst, they will be motivated to be bold for the Lord. But we as Christians are not supposed to walk by signs and wonders. We are supposed to walk by faith, not by sight (2 Corinthians 5:7). Signs and wonders follow our being bold in the Word (Mark 16:17). We should not be bold because of the signs and wonders.

The people who prayed in Acts 4:29-30 asked, **"Now, Lord, look on their threats, and grant to Your servants that with all boldness they may speak Your word, by stretching out Your hand to heal, and that signs and wonders may be done through the name of Your holy Servant Jesus."** In other words, they said, "Lord, You make us bold by stretching forth Your hand with signs and wonders." They not only asked God to do what they were supposed to do for themselves, but they went so far as to tell Him how to do it.

God responded by doing what the people asked, but He did it in a manner that they did not expect. In Acts 5:12, we read how the people's answer to their prayer actually manifested.

> **And through the hands of the apostles many signs and wonders were done among the people. And they were all with one accord in Solomon's Porch.**

God stretched forth His hand to heal, and signs and wonders manifested supernaturally. However, those signs and wonders manifested through the hands of the apostles because the only hand God uses in the earth-realm to manifest signs and wonders is the hand that Believers allow Him to use.

We need people who are bold today, who will let the Lord use them to affect people's lives for the better. For too long we have had the Milquetoast version of Christians. Too long we have had the namby-pamby preacher, the little, quiet, mousy pastor. Everyone likes him, yet he never says anything and never does anything to affect anyone's life.

God has no hands to stretch forth to heal except those in the Body of Christ. He has no mouth through which to speak and no legs on which to run errands of mercy except ours. God has designed the system so that He needs our involvement to get anything done in the earth-realm. So God will not do anything in the earth-realm without us.

God has given us *all authority* to do what He wants accomplished in the earth-realm (Matthew 28:18-20), and He has provided us with *the power* to accomplish His will through the person of the Holy Spirit within us. All we have to do is have *the will* to do what He wants us to do. What an awesome responsibility we have! And, yet, what a thrilling opportunity we have to fulfill the great commission of Jesus Christ.

Many times people wonder, "Why won't God do something?" The question may really be, "Why won't we do something?" Sometimes, we get so caught up in doing things our way that God cannot "get a word in edge-wise," as people used to say. We map out the game plan, set up the program, then want the Lord to come down and bless what we are doing. But guess what? The heavenly Father does not work that way. We have to find out how God wants us to proceed on the tasks He gives us. We have to get in line with His program, and then be bold enough to do what He wants us to accomplish in the name of Jesus and in the power of the Holy Spirit.

God has called every person in the Body of Christ to do something — and by that, I do not mean that each Christian is supposed to be an apostle, a prophet, an evangelist, a pastor, or a teacher. The Lord may ask us or lead us to do something on His behalf from time to time, and we should make sure we are sensitive to follow that leading, but whatever God may lead us to do for Him is not the primary job He has called us to accomplish in our everyday lives.

The primary task the Lord has given us is to believe, think, talk, walk, and act in line with His Word. If we do not do that job, there is no way we can accomplish whatever else God may give us. Once we renew our minds with the Word of God (Romans 12:2), get the Word into our spirits, and act accordingly, there is nothing the devil, demons, or anyone else can throw at us to stop us from prospering and being victorious in our everyday lives. Victory in our everyday lives can, in turn, help bolster our faith and boldness in anything else the Lord calls us to do.

You want to start changing people's lives for the better? Start by changing your own life. Learn to stand boldly on the Word of God to improve your situation, and it will train you to be bold in reaching out to others. And we *are* supposed to be reaching out, because that is what Jesus commissioned us to do. It is not God's will that any should perish, but that all should come to repentance (2 Peter 3:9).

Learn how to be bold in the Lord. Learn how to let the Holy Spirit work through you, and how to be a winner in life. Your blueprint is found in the Word of God. When you are a winner in life, two things happen. Number one, people want to listen to what you have to say, and number two, they are all the more interested in receiving what you and the Lord have to give them.

You want to reduce the crime rate? Get the criminals saved. You will not stop crime by hiring more police officers, making bigger locks, or giving everyone a sub-machine gun or an assault rifle. The only way you are going to stop crime is to change the criminal's heart, and the only one who can change the criminal's heart is Jesus.

The Gospel of the Lord Jesus Christ will change the hearts and lives of people if it is preached with boldness, backed up with signs and wonders, and followed by the knowledge of how to live in faith and power according to the Word of God. Once you change the heart of an individual and teach that individual how to live, you will change both that person's actions and his or her position in society. Get all the criminals born again and teach them how to live by faith, and you will not have any problems with someone breaking into your house.

We have to be bold for Jesus — just as bold as the people who are on the dance floor shaking their backsides. Be as bold for the Lord as you are when you go to a football game, a baseball game, or a basketball game. You probably holler yourself hoarse when you go to those sort of events! Be as bold for Jesus as you are with the things of the world, and you will affect the world for Christ.

Nugget No. 3

Prosperity — God's Will for You

Prosperity comes in many different forms. There is social prosperity and mental prosperity, and there is professional prosperity when God blesses the work you are doing on your job. Once you marry, you can also experience marital prosperity. There is parental prosperity in terms of raising your children, and physical prosperity in terms of your health. No Christian has a problem with any of these ways through which God can prosper us. No minister, theologian, or church denomination will tell you that any of these areas of prosperity are bad or of the devil.

When it comes to financial and material prosperity, however, that is an entirely different ballgame. When you begin to talk about those two forms of prosperity, you become a target. All of the worms come out of the woodwork, and you might even have some people talk about you. But I know the true reason these attacks come. Satan knows that if he can keep Christians poor, he can hinder the proclamation of the Gospel. And he has done a good job of keeping Christians poor, up to the present time.

It costs money to proclaim the Gospel. It costs money to build or rent a church building, to provide a pastor for a congregation, to equip a church sanctuary. Christians need an environment in which they can hear the Word, fellowship with one another, and grow in the knowledge of God.

It costs money to send missionaries to a place where no one has ever gone before with the Gospel. Also, in many of the places where these missionaries go, there is not enough financial sustenance to take care of them. Therefore, their home base or home church has to take care of them. That costs money. Who else is going to pay for the spreading of the Gospel but the children of God? Our outreach ministries are going to be based upon our financial ability to support and send those who have the call on their lives.

Satan knows that if he can keep us poor, keep us barely making it, keep us struggling to provide for our own individual households, then we will have limited resources to give to the Church. By our poverty, he can prevent us from sending out those who need to carry the message of Jesus Christ to others. Can you see that? It's a conspiracy! A person cannot give what he or she does not have, especially when the person does not know how to get it.

The world's system is not designed to aid your financial independence — not when you are a child of God. It will allow a few of Satan's kids to get wealth, so that others will think they are going to become wealthy, too. But the enemy certainly does not want the Church to become financially prosperous. That is why he has so cleverly infiltrated theology. The very people who should be supporting one another are attacking one another. We have enough opposition coming from Satan, so we do not need any coming from our brothers and sisters in Christ. When a minister or another Christian starts talking about money, non-Christians and Christians alike get on the person's case. They automatically think the minister is a crook or charlatan.

Granted, there may be some charlatans in the pulpit, but there are crooks everywhere. They are found in government, stealing from us and ripping us off. What can you say about that? Can we stop the government from operating? There are crooked doctors, crooked lawyers, crooked wives, crooked husbands, crooked children and crooked parents. There are crooks everywhere, not just in the pulpit.

I can handle what the world says, but it becomes a bitter pill to swallow when your Christian brethren criticize you for talking about prosperity. Nevertheless, we have to talk about money. This is especially true if you have a television ministry. It costs the same amounts of money to be in Christian media that it does to be in secular media. However, it would take me years to go around the world and physically teach the Word to as many people as I can reach in one hour via television. Television is the cheapest way to reach the greatest number of people in the shortest length of time, although it costs megabucks to do so.

The bottom line is, no matter what the medium a person uses, spreading the Gospel quickly boils down to dollars and cents. Therefore, if anyone ought to be sympathetic to the idea of material and financial prosperity, it ought to be Christians. We need to know how to operate in God's financial plan. As we prosper financially, God prospers in terms of our relationship to him. If we are poor, God is poor by our poverty.

Economically and financially, our world is getting worse. Yet, all the resources we need are available. Some folk are getting it and squandering it on the things that bring glory to Satan. Christians need to learn how to prosper, so that the Church can bring glory to God.

You Determine Your Prosperity

God wants you to prosper. Until you are convinced of this, you will never prosper. When you realize that Jesus and His disciples were not poor, but rather that they had wealth, you will begin to understand that you do not need to be poor to serve Him.

Joshua 1:8:

> **"This Book of the Law shall not depart from your mouth, but you shall meditate in it day and night, that you may observe to do according to all that is written in it. For then you will make your way prosperous, and then you will have good success."**

You can see it in the Word: God wants you to prosper. And the people He was speaking to were sinners. This is Old Testament, so they were not even His children; they were His servants. If God wanted His servants to prosper, you must know He wants His children to prosper.

There was a time when I did not think God liked me too well, because I am Black. It looked like all the Black folk I knew did not have very much. I thought that God just arbitrarily decided that He was going to prosper a particular man or woman, and put another man or woman on welfare. When I discovered what the Word of God said in scriptures like Joshua 1:8, I got happy. I found out at last that it was up to me whether I prospered, and that it had nothing to do with my color.

It was up to me to meditate on His Word day and night. It was my responsibility to never let that Word depart from my mouth, and to observe to do it. After I did all of that, He said I would make my way prosperous. When I discovered what God said in Joshua 1:8, I decided that I was going to be prosperous. I was going all the way. If you are willing to do it God's way, you can prosper. It's your fault if you do, and your fault if you do not.

The last part of Joshua 1:8 states, **"and then you will have good success."** This implies that there can be bad success. An example of bad success would be when you have 12 million dollars in the bank and you are driving a Rolls-Royce, but your wife is making out with the gardener, the cat raped the canary, and both of your kids are on drugs. You are up all night worrying about who is stealing from you. You cannot eat because your stomach is so ulcerated, plus you have palpitations of the heart and high blood pressure.

Good success would be having 12 million dollars in the bank, driving a Rolls-Royce, being surrounded by a loving family, enjoying a relationship with Jesus Christ, and being filled with the Holy Spirit.

Psalm 1:1-3:

Blessed is the man
   Who walks not in the counsel of the ungodly,
   Nor stands in the path of sinners,
   Nor sits in the seat of the scornful;
But his delight is in the law of the LORD,

And in His law he meditates day and night.
He shall be like a tree
> **Planted by the rivers of water,**
> **That brings forth its fruit in its season,**
> **Whose leaf also shall not wither;**
And whatever he does shall prosper.

Whatever he does shall prosper! This means that you should prosper in your marriage. You should prosper in raising your children. You should prosper in your sex life, in your professional life, in your business, in your ministry, and in your friendships. Whatever you do should prosper.

If God wanted His people poor, there should be plenty of evidence of that in the Bible. But I see just the opposite. The overwhelming evidence through the scriptures is that God wants His people to be prosperous in every way — including financially.

Psalm 35:27:

> **Let them shout for joy and be glad,**
> **Who favor my righteous cause;**
> **And let them say continually,**
> **"Let the LORD be magnified,**
> **Who has pleasure in the prosperity of His servant."**

If God gets pleasure in our prosperity, He must have displeasure in our poverty. If that is true, then God is against poverty.

The Bible tells us out of the mouth of two or three witnesses, let every word be established (Deuteronomy 17:6). I have already given you three scriptures, so I have met the biblical requirement to prove to you that God wants you to prosper in every single area of your life. Now it is up to you to do something about it. The ball is in your court.

The covers have been pulled off Satan's conspiracy to keep you poor. It is your obligation not to play into his game plan anymore.

Nugget No. 4

Name It and Claim It

Death and life are in the power of the tongue,
And those who love it will eat its fruit.

Proverbs 18:21 informs us of a spiritual law that few Christians have grasped. Yet, this scripture is, perhaps, one of the most awesome in the Bible. It can stagger the mind to realize that God has put whether we succeed or fail in life into our own hands through the words of our mouths. According to that scripture, we have authority to speak life and success, or death and defeat to our lives. It is all up to us!

The wise Christian will make a habit of making a positive confession based upon God's Word. I realize that usually in our society, the word *confession* is associated with something negative, such as confessing a crime. But in the New Testament, the word literally means "to say what God says — to agree with what God says about you."

27

This principle is so vital to the Body of Christ, yet it has been a lost principle through the years. Satan has very cleverly devised a scheme to keep it out of the Body of Christ. In fact, periodically, there are those who make fun, shoot it down, or call it false doctrine. They talk about the "Name It and Claim It bunch," referring to people like me who teach on this law of positive confession.

They call me a "Name It and Claim It" person. And I stand guilty! I am a chief exponent of name it and claim it! Oh, yeah, I believe in it. The problem is that most people do not know how to name or to claim it. So, since it does not work for them, they think it is a false doctrine, and they make fun of it.

But they don't criticize God when He says, **Death and life are in the power of the tongue** (Proverbs 18:21). It means that what you say can produce death or it can produce life. And whatever you do not name and claim, you are not going to get. So, I claim life, and I am a "Name It and Claim It" person.

The Bible says **it is impossible for God to lie** (Hebrews 6:18). Therefore, whatever God says I am, or whatever He says I have and am able to do must be true. Once I recognized this fact and began to set my life and my mouth in line with it, I began to see results manifesting in my life.

This law has operated in the realm of farming since time began — no seed planted, no crop harvested. Nobody has a problem with that. They do not call the farmers the "Name It and Claim It bunch," because they understand and accept the idea that there is a law of sowing and reaping — and that the reaping is predicated upon the sowing. No sowing, no reaping.

The same law that operates in nature also operates in the spirit. In nature, seed has to be planted in good soil and given time to germinate, grow and mature before harvesting. In the spirit, you plant your seed with your mouth — your confession. The seed you should be planting is the Word of God. Luke 8:11 tells us, **"The seed is the Word of God."**

When the farmer goes to the granary or feed store and asks for corn seed, his desire is to produce corn. He is naming and claiming it by specifying what he wants. And he does not expect to get peaches when he planted corn. When he puts corn seed in the ground, he begins telling everybody he put corn in the ground and that he is going to have a corn harvest. He is naming and claiming!

If I plant the seed of God's Word in my heart by faith and I say that I am going to have a yacht or a house or a Rolls-Royce or a new suit, why should someone get on my case? Or, if I plant and say I have good health and have healing, I am planting seed.

Luke 8:4-11:

> And when a great multitude had gathered, and they had come to Him from every city, He spoke by a parable:
>
> "A sower went out to sow his seed. And as he sowed, some fell by the wayside; and it was trampled down, and the birds of the air devoured it.
>
> "Some fell on rock; and as soon as it sprang up, it withered away because it lacked moisture.
>
> "And some fell among thorns, and the thorns sprang up with it and choked it.
>
> "But others fell on good ground, sprang up, and yielded a crop a hundredfold." When He had said these things He cried, "He who has ears to hear, let him hear!"
>
> Then His disciples asked Him, saying, "What does this parable mean?"

And He said, "To you it has been given to know the mysteries of the kingdom of God, but to the rest it is given in parables, that

'Seeing they may not see,

And hearing they may not understand.'

"Now the parable is this: The seed is the word of God."

According to verse 10, these spiritual truths are mysteries — until revealed. The critics have seen and they do not understand, but they would never admit that. So, in order to cover it up and hide their inability to perceive mysteries, they shoot the truth down and jump all over us who have learned how to interpret the mysteries. Simply because they wrote a book about their perceptions (or lack thereof), they tend to believe they are the sum total of all knowledge and wisdom.

But I cannot stop declaring the truth because someone cannot or does not want to understand what I am saying. As for the critics, I want them to get the truth of the Word because the truth is so good. I am not upset because they choose to write about me. I just hate to see them choosing ignorance and being cheated out of the blessings God wants them to have.

"Planting Seed" Works All the Time

Mark 11:12-14:

Now the next day, when they had come out from Bethany, He was hungry.

And seeing from afar a fig tree having leaves, He went to see if perhaps He would find something on it. When

> He came to it, He found nothing but leaves, for it was not the season for figs.
>
> In response Jesus said to it, "Let no one eat fruit from you ever again." And His disciples heard it.

In verse 14, Jesus is naming and claiming. The disciples heard it, so that means he spoke aloud. He did not just think this curse in His mind. He did not project an astral thought to the tree. He named it and claimed it. What He named and claimed was for that tree to never again produce fruit.

Now let us find out if the naming it and claiming it worked. Because if it worked then, it will work now.

Mark 11:20-23:

> Now in the morning, as they passed by, they saw the fig tree dried up from the roots.
>
> And Peter, remembering, said to Him, "Rabbi, look! The fig tree which You cursed has withered away."
>
> So Jesus answered and said to them, "Have faith in God.
>
> "For assuredly, I say to you, whoever says to this mountain, 'Be removed and be cast into the sea,' and does not doubt in his heart, but believes that those things he says will be done, he will have whatever he says."

In verse 23, Jesus is speaking — Jesus Christ, the Head of the Church, the Son of God, the King of kings, the Lord of lords, the Rose of Sharon, the First and the Last, He who was dead but is alive forevermore — Jesus!

31

Whoever is going to write books criticizing the principle of "saying" should write it to Jesus. Send your critique to heaven!

According to Jesus, you will have those things that you say — not things you think, nor hope, but the things you say. I did not say it — Jesus did! So, according to Him, you have to name it and claim what you desire, or you will never have it. Also, Jesus tells us, **Whoever says and does not doubt in his heart....** Now, there is the reason people criticize naming and claiming — as well as possibly the reason naming and claiming did not work for at least some of them. The critics doubt.

You can have doubt in your head and still believe in your heart that what you say with your mouth will come to pass. In fact, when you start walking by faith, you may have a lot of doubt in your head. But your head is not your heart. If you take God at His Word, He will certainly honor it. Faith will work in your heart, even with doubt in your head.

What do you believe in your heart? That is the question you should ask yourself. I do not doubt. I take God at His Word by faith, and believe in my heart that His promises are manifested in my life. I have had things I believed for while my mind was shouting and screaming as loud as it could, "It will never come to pass. It won't work. That can't happen," and my body was trembling from what my mind was saying. But God said, "Do it," and in my spirit, I said. "I'm going for it all the way." And those things I believed for came to pass, because I believed in my heart that God would do what He said in His Word.

You could say to the farmer that "whoever" plants corn and believes that he receives a harvest — all other things being equal — he will have whatever he plants. If he plants corn, that is what he is going to have. He is not going to have a peach tree. He is going to have corn. Why? Because that is what he planted. Can you see that?

It goes right back to Proverbs 18:21 — **Death and life are in the power of the tongue.** In the soil of the spirit realm, you plant seed with words. You keep talking sickness and disease and that is exactly what you are going to have.

When the farmer plants his corn seed, he tells everybody concerned that there is corn in that ground. All you can see is ground, and it all looks alike, but under part of the ground is corn seed and under another part is cotton seed. In a similar fashion, I have to tell you that there is healing and divine health in this ground; and I have to say there is prosperity in this ground, because that is what I planted. Jesus told me I would have what I say. I am telling you, you will have what you say!

On the flip side, if you are not saying anything, you are not going to get anything. Maybe that is why the critics are having the problem: they never dare to believe that the seed they planted is corn, and they are scared to say that there is corn in that ground. But the natural farmer and the spiritual farmer are not afraid, because they know what they have planted.

I started taking God at His Word — and saying it — many, many years ago, and it has been producing for me. I have claimed my housing needs to be met. I have claimed my food substance needs to be met. The Bible says that whatever you say and believe in your heart, you shall receive. Anybody who has been following my ministry for any length of time knows I have always given God, my Father, and Jesus Christ, my Lord, the credit for it all. Why would anyone want to fight that? Because they are ignorant and do not understand the mysteries of Christ. But if they would sit still long enough, shut their mouths of criticism, and listen to what I am telling them, they would learn something. Critics are listening to the devil and they do not even know it. They are doing a disservice to Almighty God without ever realizing it.

Watering Your Seed With Words

When you plant something in the natural realm, you have to continue to water until the harvest comes in. Likewise, you also have to continue to water what you have planted in the spirit realm so that your seed does not "dry up" and you receive your harvest. Too many people forget to water their spiritual crops, then wonder why the things they believed for never come to pass. They do not consider the fact that maybe they missed a step in the process.

Watering what you plant in the spirit realm is like the equation "2+2=4." Planting your seed is the first "2." Watering your seed is the second "2." If you do not put together the first "2" and the second "2," how in the world are you possibly going to arrive at "4"? You won't. Neither will you receive your blessings if you do not follow the "equation" of planting and watering your spiritual seeds.

So how do you water in the spirit? You water by using the same words you used when you planted. The way I water is to say, "I believe I receive." For instance, if I prayed for healing at 10:39 a.m. on January 26, and I believed in my heart at the time I prayed that I received what I prayed for, I would water what I planted by making the following confession: "Father God, I believe I received my healing at 10:39 on January 26. Thank you for my healing, in Jesus' name." I would also keep confessing the scriptures that pertained to my healing, as well as to its manifestation by faith, until that healing became a reality in my life.

Again, the way you say is with words. When you pray, you say words. If you did not say any words, then you did not pray. Some might say, "I have a 'silent request'." And that is what you are going to get, a "silent blessing"! Some people say, "Well, I just don't believe in saying things, Brother Price. I just believe that God knows my heart, and He knows that I have it in my heart." And God knows you're a liar! Because the Bible says, **For out of the abundance of the heart the mouth speaks** (Matthew 12:34). So, if the mouth is not speaking, it is probably because there is nothing in the heart. If there is anything in the heart in abundance, it has to come out of your mouth!

I have never preached a sermon called "Name It and Claim It." All I have done is taken God's Word and told you what the Lord said.

For the critics, if you say that naming it and claiming it is wrong, and that it is not scriptural and that it is a prostitution of God's Word, let us assume you are correct. Let us assume that confession and saying is wrong. If it is wrong, then I do not care how loud and long you say it, it is not going to work. It will produce no results! If you have a combination lock and you turn to the wrong number, you can turn the wrong numbers until the cows come home, and the lock is not going to open.

All I would ask the critics to do is prove me right or wrong on a statistical basis, because the biblical principle is that faith without works is dead (James 2:17). So, if your faith is truly faith, it ought to produce some results somewhere, sometime, somehow. All I ask of the critics is: Show me what they have produced without naming and claiming and let me show you what I have produced by naming and claiming — by taking God at His Word and giving Him all the credit and the glory. Let's get it on!

35

Nugget No. 5

Speaking What God Says

Romans 4:16-17:

> **Therefore it is of faith that it might be according to grace, so that the promise might be sure to all the seed, not only to those who are of the law, but also to those who are of the faith of Abraham, who is the father of us all**
> **(as it is written, "I have made you a father of many nations") in the presence of Him whom he believed — God, who gives life to the dead and calls those things which do not exist as though they did.**

God follows His own Word, and He demands that we be doers of the Word and not hearers only (James 1:22). He told Abraham, "I have made you a father of many nations." He was calling those things which did not exist as though they did; He was talking to Abraham as though he were already the father of many nations.

What God said to Abraham was astounding because Abraham was an old man and Sarah was well-stricken in years — past the age or time of reproduction — plus she had always been barren. You talk about "three strikes, you're out" — Sarah wasn't even on the playing field, let alone up at bat! But Abraham believed God.

There are too many Christians who read these verses and end up going off the deep end, because what they do when they read these verses is interpolate. In other words, they read something into these scriptures that is not really there. And the difference between what God is saying here and what people assume He is saying is as wide as the distance between this planet and Alpha Centauri, which is four light-years away. That means you would have to travel 186,000 miles per second — that's 66 trillion miles per hour — for four years to reach one of the closest stars to the earth.

Romans 4:17 says that God **calls those things which do not exist as though they did**; it is *not* saying that God calls those things *which do exist* as though they *did not*. It is very important to see this distinction; I am not just making a play on words. Unfortunately, many Christians have not made this distinction, and that is where they have made their mistake. They may have thought they were calling those things which do not exist as though they did, but they were actually saying the reverse, and that is an entirely different principle.

Let's take sickness and disease for an example. When Satan attacks a Christian with sickness, disease, or pain, sometimes that person will say, "I don't have any pain." Or the person comes back from the doctor after having been diagnosed with a tumor the size of a grapefruit in his or her stomach, and says, "I don't have a tumor." The pain is about to drive that person out of his or her mind, and the person is saying, "I don't have any pain." What that person is doing is calling those things that *do exist* as though they *did not,* and that is not what faith does.

Faith does not say that there is no disease. When you say there is no disease, that is when you start getting over into the philosophy practiced by Science of Mind and Christian Science. To say there is no disease is like calling God an imbecile. Do you know why? Because one of God's redemptive names is *Jehovah-rapha,* which means, "I am the Lord who heals you." How could He be the Lord who heals you if there is nothing for you to be healed of?

How can a doctor treat an illness that is not there?

Why did God say in James 5:14-15, **Is anyone among you sick? Let him call for the elders of the church, and let them pray over him, anointing him with oil in the name of the Lord. And the prayer of faith will save the sick**?

And why tell us in Matthew 8:17, **"He Himself took our infirmities And bore our sicknesses"**? How could God say in 1 Peter 2:24, **... by whose stripes you were healed,** if there were nothing to be healed of?

Pain is real. Sickness is real. Do not say that you do not have pain when you actually do. Do not even deal with the pain — deal with the cure. Speak the cure. Speak what God says.

Some people have thought they could not take any medicine or go to the doctor. They thought that by taking medicine or going to the doctor, they would be confessing something they were not supposed to admit, and so go against what God says in His Word. But they were actually mixed up as to what God was telling them. Faith calls those things *which do not exist* as though they did. Thank God that faith says, "I believe I'm healed." But if you are standing in faith against a sickness or disease, you may need medication to keep your body and your head together before your healing manifests.

Satan is banking on your acting like a fool and saying, "I don't have a tumor, I don't have any pain, I don't have this, I don't have that." He knows that when the doctor tells you that it is too late, then you are not going to go to God in faith; you are going to go to Him in desperation and fear. That fear will destroy you — and Satan is counting on it!

You should make this confession: "I thank You, Father, that Jesus took my infirmities and bore my sicknesses. I thank You that by His stripes I was healed — and since I was healed, that means I am healed and whole right now, and I believe that I am. I praise You for that in Jesus' name."

When you make that confession, you are not denying the existence of the thing the devil is using to attack you. You are saying it exists, because if it did not exist, you would not have to believe that you were healed. You are simply using your faith and the Word of God to eradicate it. It may seem like just a difference in semantics, but believe me, friend — that subtlety can be the difference between life and death.

Thank God that healing is available for us when we need it, but God's best is for us to walk in divine health — and it takes at least as much faith to walk in divine health as it does to believe in being healed. The difference is that your walking in divine health is using your faith preventively, and any doctor will tell you that it is far better to prevent a sickness from happening than it is to treat it once it manifests.

Also keep in mind that, although God moves supernaturally with gifts of the Spirit, you cannot count on the gifts to manifest your cure for you. You cannot afford to wait around for the gifts, because they manifest as the Spirit wills. God did not promise that He was going to heal everyone instantaneously by the gifts of the Spirit. We should believe in miracles, expect miracles, and desire miracles, but God did not say that the just shall live by miracles. He said they shall live by faith (Romans 1:17). So get yourself and your faith-life together.

Start saying what God says now, when you do not have any pain, when you do not have any problems, and there is nothing wrong. Build yourself up on your most holy faith so that when the enemy tries to put something on you, you will be ready and can successfully beat off that attack with the Word.

However, you will never beat off an attack of the enemy if you do not take the time to study the Word and get it into your spirit. Why don't you have time to come and hear about healing or attend healing services? Why don't you have time to study the Bible on the subject of healing? Why don't you memorize scriptures on healing? Why? Because you think you do not need them. But take my word for it — if you plan to live in this earth-realm for any length of time as a child of God, you will need those scriptures.

Do it now. Learn the Word. Do not wait until you get some pain; use your faith before you ever get there. Then when it comes, you can command it to leave in Jesus' name. I have been confessing I am healed, whole, and in divine health for over 25 years! I am building myself up a backlog of faith in my body. I am not waiting until I get pain to start dealing with it. And neither should you.

Do not fall into the trap of saying you don't have something when you actually do. That is exactly where Satan wants you.

41

While you are saying you don't have that thing, Satan is going to try to kill you with it. Do not give him that satisfaction!

Instead, say what God says about the situation. Speak the Word. Call those things which do not exist — your healing, your prosperity, your victory over whatever situation may arise — as though it were already here. By faith, stand steadfast on God's Word, and the thing for which you are believing will certainly come to pass.

Nugget No. 6

By the Spirit or by the Senses?

Many Christians walk by their senses rather than by their spirits. Consequently, they are running into a multitude of problems that will lead them down the road to defeat.

Although people may be saved and even filled with the Holy Spirit, they are not attaining and living the overcoming, victorious life. So what's the reason? It is simply because they have not made the change from the realm of the senses to the realm of the spirit.

The only way to make that change is with a renewed mind. A mind that is renewed with the Word of God is always at war with the unrenewed mind, always in conflict, always engaged in a battle with unbelief. Unbelief is simply the conflict between the spirit of a man and the senses of a man. Your senses will always demand tangible, visible evidence concerning the reality of the things of God. In contrast, the Word of God, independent of the senses, always governs the man who walks by the spirit.

It is easy to see why many Christians are falling prey to the same kinds of things that have brought non-Christians to the road of defeat. Rampant fornication, adultery, lying, maliciousness, drug abuse, and other forms of ungodly behavior result when people allow themselves to be led by their senses, by the flesh.

If the Word of God were ruling you, how could you sleep with another person's spouse? How could you use your body for prostitution? How could a spirit-ruled man or woman ravage his or her body — the temple of God — with drugs, cigarettes, and alcohol? And how could a spirit-ruled person live a lifestyle of lying and mistreating others. A truly spirit-led person could not continually behave in these ways.

The sense-ruled person is unstable, always unsure of what he has. He constantly asks for wisdom, even though 1 Corinthians 1:30 should assure him that he already has wisdom inside of him through Christ.

There is so much uncertainty in the minds of many Christians as to whether God will do what He says. They read the Bible, yet they do not believe it. It is not possible for people to really serve a God in whom they do not really believe. So they end up being moved by every situation that comes along. However they feel, that is how they respond, because they have no faith in God's Word. And going to church, in reality, is just a habit.

1 Kings 18:21-22:

And Elijah came to all the people, and said, "How long will you falter between two opinions? If the Lord is God, follow Him; but if Baal, follow him." But the people answered him not a word.

Then Elijah said to the people, "I alone am left a prophet of the LORD; but Baal's prophets are four hundred and fifty men."

The people were vacillating back and forth — sometimes following Baal and sometimes following God. They were inconsistent. *Falter* means "limp," so Elijah was telling the people, "How long are you going to limp between two opinions? If God is God, then act like it! Serve Him and be done with it. If He is not God, forget Him and go ahead and serve Baal."

That scripture is a perfect example of how many contemporary Christians behave. They do not know whether the Word of God is true or not. On Sunday mornings, many are hot to trot. On Wednesday, the same people act like they don't even know how to spell "Christ." These people feel fine as long as they are in church, the choir is singing and the pastor is ministering the Word. But when they leave that environment and go back to their jobs, where their co-workers are blowing cigarette smoke all over them, cursing all day long, and running around with one another's wives, then these Christians go back into the dumps. They don't know whether God is really real or not. They want to believe that God is, but they are not sure, because their senses keep telling them, "I don't know."

The spirit-led Christian is constant all the time.

If you want to be blessed and live the overcoming life, you have to believe God's Word and then act on what you believe.

Senses Change

The carnal man says, "You show me God, and I will believe in God." That is proof that person is operating by the senses. It does not mean that the man is not a Christian. It simply means that the man who operates in the senses is going to be a defeated Christian. He is going to be a Christian who is going to live on the ragged edge of success in the things of God, because he is going to be governed by his senses.

Senses change. They fluctuate like the weather. Therefore, if you are going to be governed by the circumstances, by the senses, you are going to live a life of confusion. Your emotions will be up and down, one day hot, one day cold. You will never experience the constant peace that is yours only as a spirit-led person.

The darkness of the sense-ruled mind is revealed very clearly in 1 John 1:1-3:

> **That which was from the beginning, which we have heard, which we have seen with our eyes, which we have looked upon, and our hands have handled, concerning the Word of life;**
>
> **the life was manifested, and we have seen, and bear witness, and declare to you that eternal life which was with the Father and was manifested to us;**
>
> **that which we have seen and heard we declare to you, that you also may have fellowship with us; and truly our fellowship is with the Father and with His Son Jesus Christ.**

In those verses of scripture, everything is sense-oriented. Everything is related to seeing, hearing, touching or feeling. There is a law that operates in the realm of the senses. In fact, we could call it the law of the senses. There also are laws that govern everything in the realm of the things of God. Look at Galatians 5:16-17:

> **I say then: Walk in the Spirit, and you shall not fulfill the lust of the flesh.**
>
> **For the flesh lusts against the Spirit, and the Spirit against the flesh; and these are contrary to one another, so that you do not do the things that you wish.**

Your flesh and your spirit are in opposition to one another. The sense-ruled Christian operates by his flesh. Your senses are located in your flesh — not in your spirit, but in your body. So, you could actually interchange the word *senses* for the words *body* and *flesh*.

The word *Spirit* in these verses is capitalized in the New King James Version of the Bible, supposedly referring to the Holy Spirit. However, I personally believe this word should not have been capitalized. There is no warfare going on inside of you between your body and the Holy Spirit. How is your body going to stand up against the Holy Spirit? I believe these scriptures refer to your recreated spirit and your flesh — that is where the warfare is going on.

Learning to Operate by the Spirit

Your mind (soul) is the mediator between your flesh and spirit. Whichever one your mind (soul) yields to will dominate your three-fold nature. If your mind is flesh-oriented, then your body will move into the realm of fleshly things. If spiritual things govern your mind, then your body is going to be channeled into and move in the realm of spiritual things.

Whenever you run into a challenge — such as whether to fornicate, lie, steal, smoke, or abuse your body in any other way — will you react in the spirit or the flesh to meet the challenge you face?

If you choose to react in the flesh, by your senses, just know that you are headed for destruction. The Bible is very clear that you will not overcome and live the life you should, if you react in the flesh. God is not flesh; He is Spirit. In order to be like Him, to respond like Him, you must develop your spirit man, so that you will react to all circumstances in the spirit only.

When the Bible speaks about the flesh, it means the senses. Your physical senses are doorways leading to your brain. You know a thing is hot because your senses tell you it is hot. You touch it and immediately a signal shoots through your body, letting you know something is hot.

What we call sins of the flesh are really sins of the senses, sins connected with the physical body. This is where you really get your problems. I have never heard of a spirit getting pregnant out of wedlock. I have sure heard of a lot of bodies getting pregnant out of wedlock! I have never heard of a drunken spirit, *per se,* a spirit overindulging in alcohol, acting irrationally. Why? Because all of these things are in the realm of the senses, the realm of the flesh.

Everything you have learned in this world has been acquired by your senses. If you were blind, it would be impossible for you to know anything visually — no color, neither light nor dark. You would be helpless in that sense. If you were to puncture your ears so that you could not hear, you would know nothing about the universe in an audible way. If you were to cut off your tongue, you would not be able to taste anything. Cut off your fingertips, and you would have no sense of touch. Stop up your nose so you could not smell, and you would know nothing about the aromas in this physical world.

Without your senses in operation, what are you going to know about the universe around you? Nothing! You are helpless and do not know anything. You can't see, hear, smell, taste or feel. You would be almost impossible to teach.

All of our school systems are designed to teach people relative to the realm of the senses. That is fine and needful. But problems arise when these people try to move into the realm of the things of God. Because people are so used to operating by their physical senses, they want to bring that same *modus operandi* into the spiritual realm that they learned to use in the physical realm. They think God is real only if they can feel, see, hear, or smell Him. So they assume that if they can't touch Him, He must not be there.

Galatians 5:18:

But if you are led by the Spirit, you are not under the law.

Those who are walking by the spirit are not walking under the law. The law only has to do with your body, not with your spirit. Jesus has given us a new law that deals with the spirit, and this law cannot be operated by your senses.

John 13:34-35:

"A new commandment I give to you, that you love one another; as I have loved you, that you also love one another.
"By this all will know that you are My disciples, if you have love for one another."

Under this new law, you will not be known by how many demons you cast out, or by how many days a week you go to church, or by how big your tithes are, or by how many auxiliaries you work in, or by how many good works you do. You will be known as a disciple of Christ if you have love for one another. This is not talking about husband and wife love, nor parent and child love. It is speaking about *agape* love — the God-kind of love.

If you wait on your senses in order to love, you have a problem. This is why there is so much strife among brothers and sisters in Christ. People are deciding whom to love based on their senses. But you have to love from the heart, from your spirit

Presenting a Living Sacrifice

The book of Galatians notes many things concerning the operation of the senses:

Galatians 5:19-21:

> **Now the works of the flesh are evident, which are: adultery, fornication, uncleanness, lewdness,**
> **idolatry, sorcery, hatred, contentions, jealousies, outbursts of wrath, selfish ambitions, dissensions, heresies,**
> **envy, murders, drunkenness, revelries, and the like; of which I tell you beforehand, just as I also told you in time past, that those who practice such things will not inherit the kingdom of God.**

This is just a partial list of things that involve the flesh. These are the kinds of things I counsel most people about. They are suffering because they are not allowing their spirit man to dominate, operate, and function. The answer to their problems is to renew their minds. And the only way to renew their minds is with the Word of God — by acting on the Word. By doing so, a person can easily conquer their senses.

It is not enough to know the Word. You must *act* on it. The Bible says that it is the doer of the Word who will be blessed in all of his deeds. Not the *knower* of the Word — but the *doer*.

Over and over, you see Christians who have been exposed to the Word; they know all of the technical data, they have their notes, tapes and books on the subject, yet they are still whipped and defeated. If the Word governed them, they would be over-comers in every situation.

Romans 12:1-2:

> **I beseech you therefore, brethren, by the mercies of God, that you present your bodies a living sacrifice, holy, acceptable to God, which is your reasonable service.**

> **And do not be conformed to this world, but be trans-formed by the renewing of your mind, that you may prove what is that good and acceptable and perfect will of God.**

Although our bodies are the universities where we learn, those of us who walk with God and walk with Christ are under a new kind of knowledge. It is called revelation knowledge — not sense knowledge. Revelation knowledge comes outside of our senses by the Word of God through the Spirit of God.

You can get information by studying the Word, but it never really becomes your information until you start living by it. Until you start winning with it! Until that knowledge is working for you, you are not benefiting from it. So the renewing of the mind involves being exposed to the Word, and programming your mind with the Word.

The man whose mind is ruled and governed by his senses is carnal; he is a "baby Christian" who will never be able to live in the fullness of those things God has provided for him. That man will be the victim of circumstances rather than the victor. That kind of man will live only on a very low level of victory in his walk with Jesus, if he experiences any victory at all.

That kind of carnal Christian is headed down the dark road to defeat. And it is an unnecessary road to travel when there is a road of victory just on the other side. Rather than continuing down that road in the wrong direction, why not change your direction, change your course in life, and change your defeat into victory.

Nugget No. 7

Your Body — Temple or Waste Dump?

There is nothing good about being sick. Sickness and disease are a part of the curse that comes because of breaking the laws of God. You can break laws and not realize it, but you are still going to pay.

You can walk off the top of a 12-story building and not know that there is such a thing as the law of gravity, but when your feet leave the top of that building, you are coming down — whether you know there is a law or not.

The good thing is that once you find out about the laws of God — or about most any other law, for that matter — and learn how to cooperate with the law, then the law can work on your behalf and not against you.

I love life! And I am learning to love it more and more, because I am finding out day by day through the Word how to prolong my life, and prolong it in good health so that I can have a healthy body, and a healthy, strong mind to give in service to the Lord. I cannot give Him any service if I am dead. But I can if I am alive.

You have to do some other things to enhance your life besides praying. Please do not get me wrong — praying is good! But you also have to learn how to take care of your body.

In America, we have a miserable way of living. It is a wonder that any of us live as long as we do. Almost everything in our society is geared towards self-destruction. It is geared towards helping the devil to kill you. In fact, he has been the instigator all along.

Our eating habits in America are abominable, atrocious. Fast food is the worst thing that ever happened to America. You may as well buy some arsenic and eat it. Fast food is killing people. It is death. And billions of dollars are being made on death. Billions!

Much of what we are doing to our bodies is out of ignorance, but the effect is still the same — sickness, disease, destruction, death!

My wife and I did not understand how bad our eating habits were. We were ignorant on matters of proper eating and the importance of regular and proper bodily elimination. Hosea 4:6 says, **My people perish for lack of knowledge.**

When the doctor told me that my wife had cancer, I was shocked. It wasn't shocking because I thought we were "too good" and that it "couldn't happen to her." That wasn't why I was shocked. I was shocked because I know the morality of the woman. I had lived with her for over 40 years. I know our stand of faith. I knew the Word of God that was in our family. I could see no reason for that kind of illness. I could see no place, no reason, neither morally nor spiritually, as to how the enemy could have an opportunity to come in.

We never thought that her eating habits could have played a part in the illness. We did not understand about the food part. We thought we were doing what was normal, what was natural. We had always eaten a certain way, and we were killing ourselves by degrees without realizing it.

Because of the fortitude of some people's bodies, they can tolerate the bad eating a little longer than others can. Others succumb to it more quickly. But most everybody is killing himself or herself by the way he or she eats. Your body is a toxic waste dump! And you know what we do with the toxic waste, don't you?

There are too many overweight people in America, fat and out of shape! Nobody really teaches us how to eat. Even the doctors in medical school are taught little about proper dietary habits. So the average person is left to do whatever he or she thinks is right. Generally, people eat whatever tastes good, without taking into consideration what it is going to do to their bodies — whether positive or negative.

But my wife and I found out how to eat. The way my wife was eating, it is a wonder she lived as long as she did. The way you eat is going to affect the way your body functions or operates. And when your body malfunctions, there is a price to pay. And it is usually progressive. But we did not know that at the time.

Ignorance Is No Excuse

I could not figure out what door we might have left open for the enemy to charge through. That was what was shocking — not that we were too good to be attacked. But I truly did not believe that the devil could get to us with something as devastating as cancer. He used major artillery! It was like ICBM missiles! It was not a firecracker. And I had no answers at the time as to the cause of the heavy attack against my wife.

1 Corinthians 6:19-20:

> **Or do you not know that your body is the temple of the Holy Spirit who is in you, whom you have from God, and you are not your own?**
>
> **For you were bought at a price; therefore glorify God in your body and in your spirit, which are God's.**

You have to not only live right morally, but you have to also take care of the temple.

All that some people do is stuff their faces! Don't tell me you don't know why you keep gaining weight. The only reason you are overweight is your eating habits. It is an absolute, historical, scientific fact that if you stop eating, you are going to lose weight. There is no way in the world you are going to gain weight if you stop eating. It is impossible.

If you stop eating, you are going to lose weight automatically. In fact, you will keep losing weight until you die if you discontinue eating. Your body will consume itself. It is going to eat something — either what you put into it, or it is going to eat itself. That is why people lose weight.

I am not fat, but my eating habits were still atrocious. So when I found out what I was doing to myself, I said, "Lord, I repent. Thank you Jesus for getting this information to me."

You can make all the confessions that you want to, but if you are not doing what you should, those confessions do not matter. If you are breaking certain spiritual laws or dietary laws, you are going to reap the results. People still die, even though they make the right confessions. My wife and I were making all the right confessions, but we were not knowledgeable in some important areas, such as eating.

We never gave a thought to the dietary area as possibly the causative factor. We were thinking the attack was purely a spiritual matter and had nothing to do with what we did physically. But we were wrong. Hallelujah and Praise the Lord that now we know! And we have begun making the necessary changes.

Now you are going to have to shape up, also. Too many people are putting undue stress on the temple. There are others who don't look fat, but they are still fat. The only reason the fat doesn't show up is that they are jogging and exercising. But they are still stuffing themselves. And if they ever stop exercising and jogging, they are going to go up like blimps.

Some of you are praying that the Lord will take away arthritis from your bodies. But if you have 10 tons of blubber hanging on your skeleton, you are bound to have arthritis. Your joints can't handle all that weight!

You might as well forget praying. There is no point in you trying to believe God for divine health. Forget it! You are not going to have it. You can't have it. It's impossible. Not the way you're abusing your body. And it's just a matter of time before the effects of that abuse show up.

Take Control Now!

You should take control of yourself now. Don't eat yourself to death. Don't continue abusing the temple of God with bad habits that will eventually cause your death. When I die, I want to leave in good health, not all crippled up and overweight because of disobedience or ignoring the laws of God. I want to leave here in the manner Jacob did:

Genesis 49:33:

> **And when Jacob had finished commanding his sons, he drew his feet up into the bed and breathed his last, and was gathered to his people.**

That's the way I want to die. I want to have all my children come around me, my grandchildren and my great-grandchildren. I'll pronounce a blessing on each one of them. Then after I finish pronouncing my blessing on them, I'm going to say, "I'm out of here! Loose me and let me go!" And I'm going to go on to glory. Just like that!

I know exactly what the devil is saying to some of you. "Suppose that doesn't work?" What difference does that make? I'm going to die anyway. I would rather go out of here believing something positive like that than to say, "Oh my God, I'm going to die in about two and a half years, what am I going to do?" Oh, no! I have to have at least what Jacob had. I have a better covenant. The Bible says we have a better covenant established upon better promises!

Don't die before your time.

Quit eating yourself to death. We have to do something to help people learn how to eat. Diets do not work! You should know that because if they did, you wouldn't have to have 25,000 different ones. *One* would be enough. There has to be a way one can lose weight naturally. And not only lose it, but maintain an ideal trim figure. Thank God there is! The key is curbing your appetite and eating live, natural, nutritious foods. You will feel better, look better, and be able to do better.

God did not create you to die before your time. He created you to live a long, healthy life. And you can live better and longer and be more effective with your life when you start changing some of your bad eating habits.

Nugget No. 8

Before You Say "I Do"

In the spring season of the year, many thoughts turn to establishing relationships, to love, to marriage. Without strong, loving relationships, there is often little meaning to a person's life. So, this is certainly an important area to discuss, especially when we see so many Christians falling prey to the same challenges and pitfalls in male-female relationships that those outside Christ face.

I want to share in this area, because I believe some of you who are either in a relationship, or are looking forward to a lasting, marital relationship, can gain some helpful insight which will be a blessing to you and your present or future partner.

Dating? Going Steady? What's It All About?

When people want to get to know someone, sometimes they think they need to get "intimately" involved. Most people use the terms *going together* or *going steady,* and they often interchange those terms with the word *dating.* However, from my understanding of *going together,* I do not believe that is the same as simply dating.

To go out to dinner, to a sporting event, to a concert, or to a movie with a person of the opposite sex is a date, to me. And I do not believe there is anything wrong with it, particularly if others are around.

But when I hear the phrase *going steady,* I understand that to be something different. I do not believe it is necessary to go steady, because I believe it could become a trap for a person, simply because the couple can get too emotionally entwined and physically involved. Just because a person goes to church on Sundays does not mean he or she is trustworthy in a one-to-one situation.

Nobody's flesh is saved and you are susceptible to the things of the flesh. So why put yourself in a situation where you can be coerced, pressured or forced into a sexual situation. You can still get to know a person to some degree by sitting and talking privately; yet the two of you can be in the same room with other people or another couple. I have walked the walk before, and it can be a trap — who needs it!

You are not going to know all the things you need and want to know about a person by going on dates or by going steady. You only get to know a person when you live with them in marriage. So, there's no need of you trying to test the waters. If you are interested in a lifetime partner, let God bring that person to you.

Why Be a Virgin?

People are so influenced by what they see on television and in movies, and too many want to do the same things in their personal lives. Too much of what we see shows couples engaging in all kinds of ungodly activities, including premarital sex. Those premarital relationships can carry over into your marriage and affect your marital relationship, because you begin to make comparisons between what was and what is now, and making those comparisons is not good.

Despite what the people on TV or the movies do, the Bible tells us clearly that premarital sex is fornication, and God does not approve of it.

1 Corinthians 6:18-20:

> **Flee sexual immorality. Every sin that a man does is outside the body, but he who commits sexual immorality sins against his own body.**
> **Or do you not know that your body is the temple of the Holy Spirit who is in you, whom you have from God, and you are not your own?**
> **For you were bought at a price; therefore glorify God in your body and in your spirit, which are God's.**

It is clear by the scriptures that we should remain chaste prior to marriage — pure, unspotted and untouched. The male should be just as much a virgin as the female. If I go to buy a new car, I want it to be a new car. I don't want it to have a thousand miles on it! That is not new. So, if a guy marries a girl who has already had five guys, that is not a new product. The same goes for the lady marrying a sexually active man.

So, you can see that some of these *alone, going together*-type situations can jeopardize your virginity.

I am very aware of the strong outside influences in the modern world that threaten a person's virginity. But even in these days, you can train up your children in the way they should go, and they will be virgins — both males and females. I have personally done it in these modern times. My three daughters were virgins when they were married, so I know it can be done.

Virginity prior to marriage is good, because it gives two people an opportunity to develop together. And I think that is really what God intended for us. There is something mysterious — in a positive way — about the interaction of a male and a female. To grow together, explore, and come to know each other in an intimate way like that is very special.

When I was growing up, my parents did not teach me these kinds of things. They had their own challenges in terms of living with each other. My father had an alcohol problem. I was often left alone. So instead of feeling like I had solace and companionship and a parent-child relationship, where I could go to my parents and talk, I felt distant and estranged from them. So, I sought the companionship of young females. But those kinds of relationships can ruin you and ruin your marital relationship.

I have seen and know about marriages that have been wrecked because of one or both partners' previous sexual experiences. In some of those relationships, you might have had one girl do all kinds of exotic things. You go into marriage thinking your wife is going to do those things that other woman did for you, and she looks at you like you're crazy! Then you get all uptight about the matter. Aside from the foremost important biblical standpoint telling us not to fornicate, those are my own observations about the problems of premarital sex.

I think that the sexual relationship is the most precious thing that a man and a woman have to give. When you give yourself sexually, what else is there left to give? Sure, you can talk, you can hug, you can kiss, you can communicate intellectually, you can share things on an experiential basis, and you can do recreational things together. But a sexual relationship is the closest relationship two people can have. It is the most personal and the most intimate.

When you give yourself to someone in that way, you have totally and completely exposed yourself. You have nothing else to hide. Sex should be treasured until you are with the person with whom you plan to spend your life.

Honesty in Relationships — A Priority

People see so much dishonesty, they think nothing of it to lie about everything. But it is so important to be honest before and after marriage. Sometimes a partner may not have been honest in discussing sexual matters with his or her potential mate, and when they get into a marriage, that partner wants to perform some kind of sexual act the other partner does not want to participate in. In such a situation, what do you do? You are already married! The number one thing you had better do is pray and seek divine guidance.

Oral sex is one of the areas where couples seem to have challenges. But just because you have the urge to do something doesn't mean it is right. A dog has an urge to lick up his own vomit, but I don't think that is a choice that a person would want to make — not an intelligent person.

If you begin looking at your body, at the organs of your body, you will see they all have purposes, and when you violate those purposes, the body cannot function properly in those areas. If you damage your ears so that you cannot hear, there is no other organ in your body that you can hear with. So, likewise, when you violate other parts of your body, there is a consequence, a price, to pay.

Think about it. What is a penis for? What is a vagina for? What is the anus for? Sure, you can put earrings on your ears, but that is not what they were made for. Ears were made to hear with. You can put a ring in your nose just as well as one in your ear. That is ornamentation, but that is not what the nose was made for. The nose was made to smell with.

When it comes to sex, or anything else for that matter, if there is any reservation, any embarrassment or feelings of guilt, feelings of unworthiness, or feelings of being dirty, we should know something is out of order. Even though we may want to do something, in the back of our mind, we know when things are not right.

There are all kinds of abnormalities, and some are not exposed until people get married. For instance, bisexuality is not the norm for humans. Because if it were, you would have more humans who are bisexual than not.

If the knowledge of such an abnormality arises after marriage of two born-again people, all of that can be overcome by the Word — if there is a will to do it, and if the couple will apply themselves to the Word. The two will really have to seek direction from God, because they will have a very serious problem in their marriage otherwise.

You could get a divorce or separate — that is the easy way out. But you never know when redemption can be brought forth. Christ died for all mankind. All situations regarding sex have to be dealt with on an individual basis.

1 Corinthians 7:12-16:

> But to the rest I, not the Lord, say: If any brother has a wife who does not believe, and she is willing to live with him, let him not divorce her.
>
> And a woman who has a husband who does not believe, if he is willing to live with her, let her not divorce him.
>
> For the unbelieving husband is sanctified by the wife, and the unbelieving wife is sanctified by the husband; otherwise your children would be unclean, but now they are holy.
>
> But if the unbeliever departs, let him depart; a brother or a sister is not under bondage in such cases. But God has called us to peace.
>
> For how do you know, O wife, whether you will save your husband? Or how do you know, O husband, whether you will save your wife?

If a person is bisexual and that person is going to practice that sinful behavior, it would be hard to believe the person was really a born-again, Spirit-filled Christian walking in the Word. Living such a lifestyle violates all the principles of God's Word. In a marriage where one or both partners act that way, it would be left to the two people to decide how they want to work it out. I do not think someone from the outside can just simply say, "Pull the plug on your marriage."

That is the kind of dilemma that one may face when there has been dishonesty in a relationship from the very beginning. If there had been honesty from the start, that marriage may not have taken place. Or at least, the other person would have had the opportunity to make a decision about it beforehand.

Honesty is the lifeblood of any marriage. It is so vital. Everything that is of concern and interest and value to the other party should be discussed before the marriage takes place. You have to talk about more than "I love you, I love you." You should talk about sex, your personal goals, and your career goals. If there is a problem area, you can then make an intelligent decision as to whether or not you should get married.

Some men do not admit their true feelings about a spouse or potential spouse earning more money than they do. That subject can be a loaded gun. If she is making more money than he is before the marriage, she will probably want to advance, and will end up making even more money during the course of their marriage. So, if a guy has low self-esteem, and he is not being honest either with himself or with her about that, he may be crushed in such a situation.

You might be saying "I love you" a lot, but you will really find out whether someone really loves you when you come up against some of these issues. Most people do not even really know what love means. *Love* and *in love* are difficult terms to understand because our society has overused, abused, misused, and misconstrued them. The word *love* has been applied to so many things that it is a word out of control.

You hear people say, "Do you want to make love?" But what they really mean is, do you want to have sex? They equate love with having sex. And you can have sex with someone that you do not ever want to see again.

Definition of Love

I have a very simple — maybe even a corny and oversimplified — definition of love. When I say, "I love you," it means I want to spend the rest of my life making you happy. I want to be your companion, your provider, your lover, your confidant, your advisor, your friend. I want you to be the only woman in the world that carries my seed and mothers my children. I want only you handling the affairs of my household. I mean that I want to spend my life with you in every conceivable intimate way that there is imaginable. I am yours for life. I want you to be mine for life. That is the best way I can define *love.*

Some people are marrying because someone says they love them and because the person is a Christian and goes to church every Sunday. But that does not mean a thing! You could still be unequally yoked. It is so important to be equally yoked in spiritual matters first. Both of you should be filled with the Holy Spirit and speaking with other tongues. You should both believe in tithing. If either one does not believe in either of these two matters, you are unequally yoked.

2 Corinthians 6:14:

> **Do not be unequally yoked together with unbelievers. For what fellowship has righteousness with lawlessness? And what communion has light with darkness?**

That scripture usually is attributed to a Christian not marrying a non-Christian. But based upon what I have been able to see from the Word and from life, I believe being unequally yoked involves some additional criteria.

If one believes in divine healing and in exercising faith to believe God for healing, along with whatever help one may be able to get from the doctor — but the other does not believe that, then you are unequally yoked.

I think you should be equally yoked on the things that mean the most to you in life. Even though you may both be Christians, you need to sit down and talk about all these other areas — with spiritual things being first.

When you talk openly, you will discover what the other likes and dislikes. My wife likes a particular food that I do not like, but it has nothing to do with our relationship. I allow her the privilege to like it, and she allows me the privilege not to. So, we are equally yoked in that sense.

Such things as whether one prefers an off-road vehicle to a regular four-door sedan can be adjusted. But if you do not agree on the spiritual matters, like tithing, you are going to have real trouble. Start with the spiritual matters, but then go on and talk about other concerns from there.

You must use honest communication; otherwise, you will be talking a lot and saying nothing. Talk about whether or not you want children. Talk about where you want to live. For example, if he likes the snow and the change of seasons and she was born in a mild tropical climate and hates snow, and he decides to move to Vermont or Connecticut where he's from, she is going to have problems — and so will their marriage. There are many areas of living that need to be discussed before a couple walks down the aisle and says "I do."

I know of a situation where after the couple was married, the lady said, "Honey, I am ready to start having children." The guy said, "What?! I do not plan to have any kids!" Now what is she supposed to do? They are unequally yoked. They should have discussed that issue until each one understood clearly where the other stood. Here, she has given herself to this guy and he doesn't want kids. That is trouble with a capital "T."

I think two people can make a relationship work under any circumstances if they agree as to what they are going to do. Some situations cannot be pre-planned, of course, but most things can.

Do all of your homework before you ever decide to get married, because you are still going to have to adjust to each other. Just the psychological and physical adjustment alone is a big responsibility. So, all the other stuff should be ironed out beforehand.

The major criteria during the spring season of romantic thoughts, leading possibly to marriage should be: Talk honestly. Get into agreement about things. Be equally yoked together. Thereafter, it is just simply a matter of putting things into operation.

The most important thing to remember is that God knows more about you than you do, so let Him in on your heart's desire. He can arrange for you to have the best life partner that you could ever imagine. Before you start your game plan, before you begin talking to him or to her, talk to your heavenly Father first!

Nugget No. 9

The Marriage Covenant

When a couple enters into union through the marriage covenant, they enter into the closest and tenderest union possible between a man and a woman. This covenant is founded on mutual affection, devotion, and commitment. For Believers, it is a union in the Lord, initiated by Him as a provision for the happiness and welfare of all mankind.

Within the marital order, God has placed the man as the head of the household — not the god of the house, but the caretaker, provider, and protector of his wife and family, just as Jesus is the Provider and Protector of the Church. This is why the Word of God says to husbands in Ephesians 5:25:

Husbands, love your wives, just as Christ also loved the church and gave Himself for her.

And to wives, it states in Ephesians 5:22-24:

> **Wives, submit to your own husbands, as to the Lord.**
> **For the husband is head of the wife, as also Christ is**
> **head of the church; and He is the Savior of the body.**
> **Therefore, just as the church is subject to Christ, so**
> **let the wives be to their own husbands in everything.**

Notice that these instructions for husbands and wives are patterned after Jesus' relationship with the Church. Some men have used Ephesians 5:22-24 to dominate their wives. Some of these men may have even dealt with their housekeepers better than they have acted toward their wives.

For a man to know how to behave toward his wife, he needs to examine how Jesus treats the Church. I have never heard of Jesus being abusive to the Church. A Christian husband should never be verbally abusive to his wife, nor beat her. When a husband strikes his Christian wife, he is striking Jesus.

Not only that, but not treating his wife properly will hinder a man's prayers from being answered (1 Peter 3:7). It also means he is not discerning the Body of Christ rightly, and not discerning the Lord's Body is an open door for sickness, disease, and premature death (1 Corinthians 11:29-30).

If the husband is taking his place in the home as Jesus takes His place in the Church, the wife need not be concerned about submitting to him. Jesus does not take unfair advantage of the Church. He does not abuse or misuse us. In fact, He is always doing something for us. He is always going the extra mile.

Paul says, in the latter part of Ephesians 5:25, that husbands are to love their wives **just as Christ also loved the church and gave Himself for her.** Love is a giving of oneself to another. In this context, it is the husband giving himself *to* his wife and *for* his wife, because that is exactly what Jesus did for the Church. If a person is a giver, there will be a time when that person is going to receive. But giving should never be based on receiving. Giving should be a motive of the heart.

Some Christian men are not giving anything to their wives; they give no time, no love, nor respect. They treat their wives like machines that are there for their own gratification and convenience — just someone to provide sex, wash dirty clothes, clean the house, take care of the children, and fix the meals. There is no real esteem shown toward their wives, nor do they make any effort to communicate with them. They will even talk to the Lord, but not to their spouses.

Men particularly need to understand that communication is a two-way street. It means listening to what your wife has to say or think. It does not mean coming home, giving her a blow-by-blow description of your day, then picking up the paper or turning on the TV when she starts to tell you about her day.

Husbands who do not effectively communicate with their wives do not usually receive revelation knowledge from them. God can give a person wisdom from anyone or anything He chooses. If a husband continuously refuses to receive spiritual revelation from his wife, I believe he is asking for trouble.

1 Peter 3:1-8:

> **Wives, likewise, be submissive to your own husbands, that even if some do not obey the word, they, without a word, may be won by the conduct of their wives,**
>
> **when they observe your chaste conduct accompanied by fear.**
>
> **Do not let your adornment be merely outward — arranging the hair, wearing gold, or putting on fine apparel —**

rather let it be the hidden person of the heart, with the incorruptible beauty of a gentle and quiet spirit, which is very precious in the sight of God.

For in this manner, in former times, the holy women who trusted in God also adorned themselves, being submissive to their own husbands,

as Sarah obeyed Abraham, calling him lord, whose daughters you are if you do good and are not afraid with any terror.

Husbands, likewise, dwell with them with understanding, giving honor to the wife, as to the weaker vessel, and as being heirs together of the grace of life, that your prayers may not be hindered.

Finally, all of you be of one mind, having compassion for one another; love as brothers, be tenderhearted, be courteous.

Notice, in the seventh verse it says, **... as to the weaker vessel, and as being heirs together of the grace of life.** This verse is addressed to both Christian men and women. Many people think Peter is talking about a Christian woman and an unsaved man, but that is not the case here — although verse one tells how a Christian woman who is married to an unsaved man can win her husband over to the Lord.

According to these verses, husbands are to honor their wives (even though they are considered the weaker vessels) **as being heirs together of the grace of life.** God's supreme plan for the marriage covenant is that the husband and wife be one flesh, and heirs together of His grace. When a husband realizes this fact and accepts God's plan, his prayers will not be hindered. He will have free access to God, and his union with his wife will be the kind of union that God wants it to be.

The Bible clearly emphasizes that the husband is to be the head of the family. If he is not, the wife should help him to become that head. Her helping him will make her life better and what it ought to be.

1 Corinthians 7:3-4:

> **Let the husband render to his wife the affection due her, and likewise also the wife to her husband.**
> **The wife does not have authority over her own body, but the husband does. And likewise the husband does not have authority over his own body, but the wife does.**

The relationship between a husband and wife is a 100-100 percent proposition. They are both supposed to relate equally to one another.

A very important part of a husband and wife's maintaining an equal relationship is stated in 1 Corinthians 7:5:

> **Do not deprive one another except with consent for a time, that you may give yourselves to fasting and prayer; and come together again so that Satan does not tempt you because of your lack of self-control.**

Deprive in this context simply means you should not withhold your body from your husband or wife sexually. Too often, husbands and wives deprive one another as a means of retaliation. Some wives do not want to be bothered, so they stay in the kitchen half the night, fooling around with things and hoping their husbands will have gone to sleep before they get in bed. Neither of these situations is right.

As far as I can tell from this scripture, the only legitimate reason a husband or wife has for denying his or her body to one another would be if he or she wants to go into a period of fasting and prayer. In this case, they are not supposed to defraud one another unless they both consent, and then only for a time, to avoid Satan's temptation to marital infidelity.

Making sure you do not unduly deprive your spouse is another area where communication is essential. If you do not know how to talk to one another, how are you going to be able to get into consent? How are you going to agree together to fast and pray if you are not communicating?

If you and your spouse are having a challenge with maintaining a smooth relationship in your marriage, then you need to start effectively communicating with one another. You need to start talking about whatever concerns you — including your sexual intimacy, particularly if there is a problem there. The sexual union is even better when a couple communicates well.

Another factor that can enhance a husband and wife's sexual intimacy is when they are both filled with the Holy Spirit, because then there exists a greater capacity to appreciate the physical body as being the temple of God. The heavenly Father does not view the Believer's body as some little shanty with a tin roof down by the riverside, or as an outhouse. He views it as a beautiful and holy place. In the covenant of marriage, He also views the body as belonging to the spouse.

God has so united matrimony with human life that man's deepest interest revolves around this institution. When a man and a woman have chosen each other, and come to that moment when they sincerely and publicly join in the marriage covenant, they lay down on the altar a holy sacrifice to God, to each other, and to humanity. As they follow the Father's divine order, they find true and lasting happiness, as they love, honor, and cherish one another as to the Lord.

Nugget No. 10

Divorce —
Only You Can Decide

If you are married, a Spirit-filled Christian, and contemplating divorce, you need to pray about it first and be led of the Holy Spirit as to what is best for you. Be very sure about your decision before taking this course of action.

Before taking this step, make sure you sit down and discuss this matter with your spouse. Divorce is a life-changing situation. Sometimes hasty decisions are made to dissolve a marriage when, in fact, the circumstances could have been resolved.

There is a rash of divorces among Christians at the highest levels. And these divorces seem to be opening a Pandora's box, so to speak, that is making it easy for other Christians to believe it's okay to get a divorce, too. They are saying, "Well, if so-and-so can get a divorce and he [or she] is a preacher, then I know it's not wrong for me to divorce my mate."

That kind of thinking is silly. Just because marriage did not work for one person does not mean it cannot work for you. Stop looking at other people — no matter who they are, and keep your eyes on the Word of God. Keep your eyes on the covenant that you and your spouse made between each other — and God!

I believe that God's ideal is that you get married and stay married to that one person all of your life. But you cannot be intelligently married to someone if you do not know all the facts about marriage.

If you had properly assessed your potential partner and the situations in your relationships prior to marriage, you probably would not even need to be considering a divorce. Of course, many people do change during the course of a marriage. Some change for the better, and others for the worse. Lots of things can arise that you really could not foresee in the beginning, such as physical and emotional abuse, drug and alcohol abuse, and infidelity.

But are you obligated to spend your life in misery, with a monster who beats and abuses you? In such cases, I would like to say, "Divorce the monster!" But that is a decision that only you can make.

Situations of such severe abuse could mean your death, or the death of your children. Even the emotional torment in a marriage can be devastating. And I do not believe God wants you to be miserable and unhappy and endangered all of your life.

Matthew 19:6 says, **"So then, they are no longer two but one flesh. Therefore what God has joined together, let not man separate."** Many people are confused by that scripture, including many in the pulpit. As a result, there are folks living in bondage to their rigid church doctrine about the stigma of divorce. Meanwhile, they live a life of torment, tears, and danger.

In many of these kinds of situations, God did not have anything to do with putting the persons together. The people put themselves together. And that is why some people are suffering, living with somebody who has never grown up, never changed, or staying evil until he or she is 80 years old!

God Hates Divorce

When Jesus mentions **"...let not man separate,"** I believe He is talking about the institution of marriage. If you read that wrongly, it seems as though God will put people together against their will. But God does not violate our will.

2 Corinthians 3:6:

> **who also made us sufficient as ministers of the new covenant, not of the letter but of the Spirit; for the letter kills, but the Spirit gives life.**

God hates divorce, but He also does not want you hurting. Do not get into bondage if you are already divorced or if you are contemplating divorce from a situation that you find life-threatening and full of misery. Whether you are divorced or not has nothing to do with your salvation. It is something that only you, your spouse, and the Lord really know all about.

If you have actually made a decision to get a divorce, then there is not much anybody can say to stop you anyway. When your relationship gets to that point, obviously you believe you have already exhausted all the reconcilable areas of the relationship.

The reason you split up is that you "cannot" live together. Or you won't live together. So, the natural sequence is to officially break it off. If you have chosen this course of action and you have children, you have so many things to take into consideration. Who is going to get the kids, the property, etc., etc.

The reason people come to the point of divorce is because they don't get along. They're at odds, which means they are in disagreement about some issues. It could be a thousand things. But for many of these areas of disagreement, if they had been settled prior to the marriage, there would have been no reason for divorce later.

Most issues of divorce and marriage are tied into the areas of communication, honesty, sex, and money. If the husband and wife are not communicating, they are not going to be able to get into agreement.

Some people believe they should stay together for the sake of the children. But that's crazy. It's ridiculous. Suppose both of you had a heart attack and dropped dead — what's going to happen to the kids? They're going to survive! They still have their lives to live. If you are not happy, the kids are not going to be happy.

And happiness, of course, is based upon getting into agreement. You have to discuss areas of disagreement. I believe if you do that in the beginning, you will never get to the divorce.

When negative situations begin to happen in a marriage, there might not be a lot you can do. For example, in the case where lies have been told, there is no way you would know someone is lying unless the Holy Spirit reveals it in some way. All you can go by is what the other person is saying. In the natural, marrying someone is a gamble.

But I believe that in the realm of spiritual values, if we deal honestly with those spiritual aspects first, the rest of it is automatic. In other words, if you put God first, your marriage can work no matter what the two of you come up against.

Many people in Christian circles say there is an attack on Christian marriages. I don't know if that is an accurate statement. If my wife and I agree on the basic life considerations, how can we be attacked? The only way that could happen is if there is some division or a break in the relationship already.

When people say there is an attack on the family, they are giving Satan a lot of credit he doesn't deserve. Satan is not the one who determines whether a Christian marriage and family stay together or not.

Let me give you an example: If I sat down and ate a full-course meal and ate so much I was about to burst, and someone walked through the door with five little four-wheel carts loaded with all kinds of food, that would be no temptation to me. You couldn't attack me with that.

Where I could be attacked with food is if I'm starving and I haven't had anything to eat in seven days! Now, you can attack me. And anything you bring in here to eat is going to be a possible temptation to me.

The point is, Satan cannot attack you unless there is something to attack. Something has to already be going wrong. Even so, he's not attacking you as much as he is just assisting you in self-destruction. We are really the ones who destroy the relationship. If Satan could destroy it, what's the point in following the Word? Why do we need to be filled with the Spirit? Where is God in all this if the devil can just rip it apart?

All the devil can do is tempt us, but he cannot tempt us unless we are already at a point of dissatisfaction and disagreement. If our relationship is good, there is nothing he can do to break it up.

When Christian divorces are publicized all over the media, the only thing Satan is doing is taking advantage of something we are doing.

The Christian community sometimes repeats little catch phrases that are not necessarily true statements. And this statement about there being a "recent attack on the Christian family" is one of those little phrases. The truth is that Satan has been attacking the family since the Garden of Eden. I don't think he has ever let up on the attacks throughout history!

But his so-called attacks have nothing to do with whether my wife and I or you and your spouse stay together. For instance, if you have a flak jacket on and I sit here with a .45 caliber automatic and just keep pumping bullets at you, that is not going to hurt you. But if you don't have any protection and I shoot you, you're dead!

What I am saying is that all Satan does is take advantage of an already bad situation. He's always alert to our weaknesses or our unwillingness to do it God's way.

In Marriage, Somebody Has to Yield

The devil cannot destroy us without our cooperation. We are all really destroying ourselves. All Satan is doing is assisting us, and seeing to it that whatever we are involved in becomes a royal mess by the time he is through with his meddling. He is an agitator. However, his agitation cannot mess us up if we have a relationship based upon a solid foundation. When two people are fighting and butting against each other in a marriage, if you look closely, you will see that it is really selfishness on the part of one or both of the parties involved.

At an intersection, if both cars decide they are going through the intersection at the same time, there will be a wreck. Somebody has to yield. In a marriage, the reason the couple messes up is because neither one wants to yield. Both spouses are determined to have the right-of-way.

There is always a lot of confusion when selfish people do not yield. If I refuse to yield and you refuse to yield, nothing will work. This is an act of our wills. I do not care how much Word you know — if you do not and are not willing to apply the Word, the Word by itself is not going to change the situation. The Holy Spirit cannot change things if you are not willing.

In my own case, the thing that kept my wife and me together was that we both wanted to please God. She could have easily divorced me and found somebody else, because I was an immature fool. She had all kinds of legitimate reasons to divorce me. I did not beat her or get drunk and stay out all night, but I made her life hell on earth. I would make one decision one minute and change it the next. She could not depend on me. And because I was always changing and making bad decisions, I was dragging her through a lot of mess.

But we had a purpose bigger than our own selfish purposes. And that was to please Jesus to the fullest extent that we knew. We were both devoted and committed to Jesus.

In the early years of our marriage, we did not know the Word, but my conversion was very real to me, and her relationship to God was very real to her. And that is what kept us together until we could grow in the Word and start applying the Word to the deficient areas in our lives.

In other words, Jesus was first. With most couples, he says he's first or she says she's first. Jesus is not first. They're first, and that is when they break up. But because of our desire to please the Lord and let Him be first in our lives and knowing that divorce is certainly not the will of God, we stayed together. By our staying together, we gave our relationship time to mature. Maturity develops over time. Although you may have good potential for maturity, it will never develop if you do not allow enough time for it to do so.

Thank God we got ahold of the Word. Some people have time but never get the Word, so they end up being miserable their whole married life. But once we got ahold of the Word, discovered the reality of the Word, and began giving the Word first place in our lives, the Word and faith changed things! Through what I did with the Word, I was able to change my shiftless, undependable, unfocused lifestyle.

I used my faith and became stable, dependable; my word became good, and I became more disciplined in many areas of my life. I became a good father; in the past, I had wanted to forget the responsibility of fatherhood. Fatherhood is an awesome responsibility, but I took my faith and developed myself into a fairly decent husband and father.

If you are willing, you can turn things around in your marriage by applying the Word. That divorce you are contemplating just might not be as necessary as you think.

Think about it. Only you can make this very important decision.

Nugget No. 11

Family —
Your Greatest Asset!

Unity in the family of God is of utmost importance to our heavenly Father. His heart's desire is that we be one; that we love each other; that we encourage each other; that we fellowship with each other and that we come to each other's aid. By doing these things, we become a stronger, more powerful entity in this earth-realm. Only through that unity can we really rule, reign, and advance in royalty.

One thing that is intimately connected to this idea of unity is that, as the minister and his family go, so goes the church. The minister and his family should be a replica of the Body of Christ, with Jesus as the head and all of us as family members in the Body of Christ. Spiritually speaking, if the minister does not have his family together, if he does not have his life together, it is going to show up in his ministry. He cannot suppress it. It is going to leak out and your congregation is going to become a reflection of whatever the minister really is.

When there is dissension, hard feelings, envy, selfishness, a struggle for power and all other manner of evil within the Christian family, God cannot operate as He would like to in that family, nor can He operate in the Body of Christ. It does not matter whether those negative things come into the Body through the pastor, his family, or anyone else in the congregation. God cannot manifest His works through a Body that is filled with garbage! The flow of His Word is thwarted, and many lives are lost to sin, sickness, and poverty — lives controlled, in effect, by our archenemy, Satan.

Recently I have had to deal with ministers, stalwart men in the things of God, who have taken a misstep and faltered in their onward progress. The fact that these ministers faltered has, in turn, adversely affected people in their respective churches. Ministers of the Gospel cannot afford to play games, yet I know too many ministers who are doing just that.

Ministers especially have a tremendous responsibility to walk by the Word, not by what the world allows. They represent Almighty God, and His Son, Jesus Christ, in this earth-realm, and they have a mandate from Him to be what they preach. They ought to be so transparent that the world can look right through them! Too many ministers are playing roles, as if they are in an acting career. These preachers need to realize and get into their spirits that they are not taking a screen test. They are in the real world!

Part of living in the real world is being cognizant of the fact that all of us — ministers and laypeople alike — are supposed to be examples to the world on how to live, since we are supposed to let our light so shine before men (Matthew 5:16). The Body of

Christ is a model for how our individual families should operate. And the Christian family should set the standard for families in general. The lifestyle of our families should not mimic that of the world, but rather, that of the Family of God.

Likewise, no book can adequately instruct the non-Christian man or woman how to be a good spouse or a good parent. For the most part, it is just get in there, and sink or swim. Unfortunately, too many people sink! But Christians, you do not have to sink! Christians, you do not have to follow the ways of the world. We have the Word of God!

Paul tells us in the first part of 1 Corinthians 10:13 that no temptation has overtaken us except such as is common to man. Nearly all of us have lived in families. Chances are that most of us will marry and raise families of our own. And all of us will certainly be tempted.

The fact of the matter is that we are in a spiritual warfare. We have a relentless enemy who is out to destroy the Body of Christ in the earth-realm — the Church. All Satan has to do is destroy the man in the pulpit, and then he has the pew. I know of churches right now that because of the pastor's falling, the congregations are falling.

Don't Let Your Ego Get out of Hand

Ministers, you do not have to sink — not if you let the Word of God be the final authority in your household! And remember, God would not call you to the ministry to neglect your first ministry, which is your family! If it does not work at home, then forget it; it is not going to work in the pulpit!

The enemy is devouring many of our Christian families because we are not practicing what we profess to believe. As I mentioned before, even many ministers do not personally apply the Word of God that they teach! How sad! They counsel others, but do not take their own counsel. The result is that their households are going to pot while they are saving the world, and that should not be! I encourage you to take a personal assessment of your own home and make the necessary changes — now!

For instance, you have to use wisdom and stay away from situations you know you cannot handle. Do not spend too much time alone with the opposite sex for business, lunch, or anything else. It is just not good policy, and you do not need to be put into a place of temptation. That is why things need to be right in the home. It is hard to be tempted with food after you have already eaten until you are about to burst. No food looks good then. But if you are starving, almost any type of food looks desirable. The same principle holds true when it comes to your personal life. If you are happy and satisfied at home, "Esmerelda Brown" does not hold out too much temptation for you!

Sometimes women put their husbands in a bad situation. Sometimes it can be partly the man's fault, because he does not know what he is doing. I have almost been tempted to have some classes on how men should treat their wives sexually. Most people have learned about it from the street or the movie screen, when they should have learned it at home.

Another situation to avoid is when ministers go one place to minister, and their wives go to another place to minister at the same time. That is not the way God designed your family or your ministry to operate. I take my wife nearly everywhere I go. I am not going anywhere by myself, because those hotel bedrooms are lonely at night! I don't want to go anywhere without my wife. I want her with me. I am very suspicious of men and women in ministry who are always going someplace to minister without their mates. You should not leave yourself open to such temptation; you are not built to handle it.

And all these women calling you on the telephone. Cut it off! Don't let your ego get out of hand. If you have a wife, that is all you need. That is all you can handle. If you are taking care of her like you should, she will take up all of your time. And if your wife is not handling things, maybe you need to teach her or maybe both of you need some lessons.

The devil has people planted in some churches just to bring ministers down. He does not play fair. He will use anything he can to bring you down. He will use the lust for power, position, money, and he will use females.

If anybody is going to be right and for real, it ought to be the man who is preaching the Word of God. If he fails, what do the people have left? Jesus is not here in the earth-realm; they cannot see Him and follow Him around as a role model like Peter, James, and John could. They have to follow other men who claim to know Christ and have been called and ordained by Him. If you claim to be called and ordained by the Lord, then you ought to be about the Man's business. You should not be about your own agenda.

Do not sacrifice your family for your ministry. God instituted the family before He established the Church. Your priority should be God first, then your family, and then your ministry. Always be sure to do something special with your wife and kids. Take vacations. Take a day off. My kids can never say I was so busy in ministry that I did not have time for them. I shared my ministry with them. They since have encouraged my wife and me to do some things that the Lord directed us to do, because they never felt neglected.

You might want to take your family to Hawaii, but you may not have the money. It is commendable that you want to do that. But what we used to do was to take the kids to the grocery store, buy some salami, cheese, saltine crackers and soda, and just drive some place and have a picnic. It was a lot of fun. That was quality time together. The kids knew we loved them, and I wasn't always gone some place ministering.

You also need to be alone with your spouse. Take a weekend to just spend some time together. You ministers who are too busy for your wives and never have time for vacations are not following the Spirit of God. You are following the spirit of the devil. The Bible says that one day the disciples were out ministering. When the disciples returned, Jesus told them to come aside for a while, because they were coming and going so much that they didn't have time to eat (Mark 6:31). That can happen to you, too, if you let it, because the needs of the people are always there.

I believe that ministry and family are compatible. I do not believe God calls a man to ministry and makes him make a choice between his family and serving the Lord. That is not biblically accurate. As I have stated, God would not call you to the ministry to neglect your first ministry, which is your family. If your "ministry" does not work at home, forget it — it is not going to work in the pulpit. Some pastors want a big church because they think a big ministry means success, and that is not so.

You Must Be a Man of Prayer

There are ministers running around to all kinds of meetings. They are not there to receive anything spiritually; they are there to find out about a new gimmick, or to figure out how to make their churches grow. They are not about God's business, but about their own business. They are so busy running from meeting to meeting that they do not even have time to pray. And you must be a man of prayer.

Ephesians 6:18:

> **praying always with all prayer and supplication in the Spirit, being watchful to this end with all perseverance and supplication for all the saints.**

If you look at Jesus, you will see that He spent much of His time in prayer. So the man of God, the minister, also has to be a man of prayer. Ephesians 6:18 means that we should pray with all kinds or types of prayer. There is more to praying than "My name is Jimmy, I'll take all you gimme!" There is more to prayer than just petitioning for one's self— "I want a new car," "I want a new house," or "I want a bigger piano." Of course, petition prayer has its place, but there is also the prayer of intercession, prayer of agreement, prayer of worship, and prayer of praise.

Prayer needs to be a part of your life, whether you are a minister or a layperson. You ought to start your day with prayer! I know many folks are not praying because they are too involved, too busy. There are ministers too busy ministering to pray! And read the Bible? What's that?! They are more concerned with going to another committee meeting. Personally, I don't allow myself to get that busy. I just don't allow it. I stay in control of my schedule.

You have to take time to pray. You have to make yourself do it. You do not pray because you feel like praying, because most of the time, you will not feel like it. Prayer is not an emotional involvement; it's a spiritual exercise that you should do because the Word of your Father tells you to pray *always* — not just in tight situations, or when the roof is caving in on you. Not when the members are leaving so fast you don't know how you are going to pay the mortgage on the church building. No! The Bible says to pray always with all prayer.

1 Thessalonians 5:17:

pray without ceasing.

A man who fortifies himself with prayer is a man who will be able to stand when the enemy comes at him like a flood. You have to be regimented, disciplined, to make yourself pray. I do not pray because I get a feeling. I pray because there are results I know that are forthcoming which I believe I will see in my life, in my ministry, and especially my family.

Be an Example

The family prospers by the same measure they see at home, in our lives. That's the real test. The pulpit is not the test. It's the home. All of my children are saved and filled with the Holy Spirit. They are all involved with the ministry — at their request, not mine. I did not have to drag them to the ministry to get them involved. They came voluntarily because they saw something real in Mommy and Daddy. They saw me in the pulpit, on TV, and in the house. They know from personal experience that once you have seen me one place, you have seen me in all places. I am the same all the time, and my children saw that.

God wants you to be yourself at all times, not one way in the pulpit and another way at home. When I hear some people in the pulpit talk, some of what I hear those people say makes me want to vomit, because I know what they are saying is fake. It's phony. Just be yourself. If you do not like yourself, change. But don't be phony.

1 Timothy 3:2, 4, 5:

> **A bishop then must be blameless, the husband of one wife, temperate, sober-minded, of good behavior, hospitable, able to teach;...**
>
> **one who rules his own house well, having his children in submission with all reverence**
>
> **(for if a man does not know how to rule his own house, how will he take care of the church of God?).**

According to verse two, you should have good behavior — and good behavior does not mean sleeping with someone else's spouse! We have to be what we preach or we need to stop preaching. The world does not need to see any more ministers fall. If you do not have a handle on your life, get out of the pulpit until you get it together. Do not bring reproach on the Lord.

Moreover, verse five says that if you don't know how to take care of your home, how are you going to take care of your church? That might be why the Lord doesn't allow your ministry to get any bigger than it is — because He cannot trust you. You do not have your house together, so if He gives you any more people, it would kill you and them too. He does not need any more sacrificed sheep.

Ministers need to be an example in the word they speak as well as in their whole manner of living. Too many ministers have no integrity whatsoever. The sheep will play ministers against each other. They get mad at Fred because Fred won't let them have their way, so they go to a church that takes them right in and lets a disgruntled person become involved in leadership. A minister should not want someone else's disgruntled member involved in leadership, because there will be problems eventually.

A minister has to be a man of integrity, and that starts in your own house, with your own spouse and children. If you tell your children you are going to do something, you need to do it. If you don't, your word loses all credibility right there in your house, and that will flow over into your ministry. I am a man of my word. I have worked very diligently over the years to preserve my word and it means a lot to me. That is why I seldom make promises. If I give my word, I have to keep it.

Some jive-time ministers do not keep their word. They do not take into consideration that the Lord is watching them, and their recording angels are taking notes! They think they are pulling something off because they are fooling the people. But they are not fooling anybody but themselves, and their deception is going to come out eventually. God doesn't settle every Friday night. Payday is not every week with God. The wheels of divine justice grind ever so slowly, but they grind ever so finely.

Ministers! Remember that your public ministry is a reflection of your home ministry. Many ministers are living one way at home and putting on a performance in the pulpit. That is not going to cut it. The devil will expose you. You have no covering, and God cannot protect you in that kind of environment.

Don't ever get to the place where you think you have all the answers. You have some, but teach the people to call on God, instead of calling you all the time. My responsibility as a minister is to give the people what God has given me. I give them the best I can and if that doesn't help, then they have to appeal to the Higher Source.

If you walk in the integrity of God's Word, you will have the solution to the people's problems and you will not become a part of the problem. There is only one solution to all problems — just one — and that is the application of the Word of God. Learn to turn all your problems over to the Lord. Then you will be on the road to true success in ministry and home.

Nugget No.12

Jesus — The Resurrection

Resurrection Day, or "Easter Sunday," is the day we traditionally celebrate the resurrection of the Lord Jesus Christ. I believe it to be the most important day on the Christian calendar because everything in Christianity hinges on the reality of the resurrection. If the resurrection of the Lord Jesus Christ is not a literal fact, then Christianity is nothing other than one of the great religions of the world.

1 Corinthians 15:20-22:

> **But now Christ is risen from the dead, and has become the firstfruits of those who have fallen asleep.**
> **For since by man came death, by Man also came the resurrection of the dead.**
> **For as in Adam all die, even so in Christ all shall be made alive.**

Jesus Himself said, when He appeared in a vision to John on the Isle of Patmos:

Revelation 1:8:

> **"I am the Alpha and the Omega, the Beginning and the End," says the Lord, "who is and who was and who is to come, the Almighty."**

Traditionally, most denominations have accepted and followed the "fact" that Jesus died on Friday. This and many other "facts" surrounding the event known as "Easter" are inaccurate and unscriptural, even though most traditional churches have accepted them. I believe that Christians ought to know the truth and the fact that the resurrection of Jesus Christ does not have a thing to do with chocolate-covered rabbits or other such trappings.

We know that at a certain point in history, Jesus walked the earth. He was God manifested in the flesh, the invisible God who came down into the realm of visibility so that man could see Him. Jesus said repeatedly throughout His ministry, "Whoever has seen me has seen the Father." In other words, "I am God manifested in the flesh so you can see and comprehend what God is all about. If you are looking for the Father, look at Me."

Satan thought he could destroy Christianity by destroying Jesus. That is the reason he put the idea of betraying Jesus to the Pharisees into the heart of one of Jesus' own men, Judas Iscariot. Then the Roman government, acting on false charges against Jesus, killed Him.

After the crucifixion of Jesus, the devil realized that persecution would not stop Christians. The more he persecuted the

Church, the more the Church grew. The more he put pressure on the Body of Christ, the bolder we got; and the more he tried to stop us, the louder we preached. So he decided on another tactic — to water down and compromise Christianity.

Satan had an open vessel in one of the great emperors of antiquity, Constantine, who made an edict establishing Christianity as the state religion. Because of this decree, it suddenly became fashionable to be a Christian. Government leaders, soldiers, and many others began to come into the Church. The church leaders of the day, desiring to make the people happy, began to compromise the pure doctrines of Jesus and His Apostles.

This is how the word *Easter* got into Christianity. The word *Easter* is not found in the Bible. In Acts 12:4 the word that is translated *Easter* (in the King James Bible) is the Greek word *pascha* meaning "Passover." It does not mean *Easter*.

The word *Easter* comes from *Astarte,* the goddess of fertility. Bunny rabbits are symbolic of fertility because they are prolific reproducers. Spring is a time when the earth is coming back to life from winter, when the greenery is coming forth. Many pagan rituals were celebrated at that time, and these pagan rituals and traditions were lumped together with the resurrection, watering it down. The resurrection is Christian, but Easter is not.

Good Friday is supposed to be the day on which Jesus was crucified. Yet, Jesus said He would be in the heart, or the belly, of the earth three days and three nights. Dear friends, there is no way you can pull out three days and three nights from Friday night to Sunday morning. I do not care how much of a mathematician you are. Still, many Christians go along, year after year, following this fallacy.

A God of Accuracy

The God we serve is a God of accuracy. And Jesus Christ is not a party to confusion. Either He was or He was not in hell for three days and three nights. And we ought to be able to find that out in the Bible.

Matthew 27:62-66:

> **On the next day, which followed the Day of Preparation, the chief priests and Pharisees gathered together to Pilate,**
>
> **saying, "Sir, we remember, while He was still alive, how that deceiver said, 'After three days I will rise.'**
>
> **"Therefore command that the tomb be made secure until the third day, lest His disciples come by night and steal Him away, and say to the people, 'He has risen from the dead.' So the last deception will be worse than the first."**
>
> **Pilate said to them, "You have a guard; go your way, make it as secure as you know how."**
>
> **So they went and made the tomb secure, sealing the stone and setting the guard.**

These chief priests and Pharisees were Jesus' detractors. They were opposed to His ministry. Yet out of their own mouths, they repeated what they had heard Jesus Christ, Himself, say.

There are two terms which need to be clarified — *Resurrection* and *raised from the dead*. It is one thing to be raised from the dead, and quite another thing to be resurrected.

When Jesus says in John 11:25-26, **"I am the resurrection and the life. He who believes in Me, though he may die, he shall live. And whoever lives and believes in Me**

shall never die...," He is talking about spiritual death and spiritual life. He does not mean that, if you believe in Him, you are not going to physically die. Some people have misconstrued what Jesus said and have gone out teaching a doctrine that you are not going to die. The Bible does not say you are not going to die physically. The Bible says in Hebrews 9:27, **And as it is appointed for men to die once, but after this the judgment.** How could Jesus be talking about physical death when He says, **"He who believes in Me, though he may die, he shall live."** Paul died. Peter died. Stephen died. Jesus was talking about real death, which is spiritual.

So, what is the difference between being raised from the dead and the resurrection? Jesus had just raised Lazarus from the dead, but Lazarus, unfortunately, had to die again. The widow of Nain's son, who was raised from the dead, had to die again, as did Jairus' 12-year-old daughter, whom Jesus also raised from the dead. Resurrection, however, is when you cannot die anymore; death has no more hold on you. Jesus is alive today because He was resurrected.

Romans 6:9:

knowing that Christ, having been raised from the dead, dies no more. Death no longer has dominion over Him.

Now, let us look closely at Jesus' statement, **"After three days I will rise."**

Mark 15:42:

Now when evening had come, because it was the Preparation Day, that is, the day before the Sabbath,

Religious tradition gets the idea that Jesus died on Friday because verse 42 says, **... the day before the Sabbath.** To most people, the Sabbath is every Saturday, so the day before the Sabbath would be Friday. However, Jesus very clearly said that the only sign He would give would be **"three days and three nights in the heart of the earth."** Preparation on Friday could not possibly be true because you cannot add three days and three nights to Friday and still end up on Sunday.

Go back to Mark 15:42, and notice the words *Preparation* and *Sabbath*. John 19:14 reads, **Now it was the Preparation of the Passover....** This is referring to the very same event that is recorded in Mark's Gospel — only in the latter account, the Holy Spirit specified what Sabbath the preparation was for. It was not the preparation of the weekly Sabbath, but the preparation of the Passover Sabbath.

The Passover is a Sabbath day. In fact, the Jews had more than one Sabbath day, which has caused confusion. All these days that were considered Sabbath were all to serve the same purpose — to have the people rest. They were all to be called days of rest. But there were several different ones.

Leviticus 23:1-2:

> **And the LORD spoke to Moses, saying,**
> **"Speak to the children of Israel, and say to them:**
> **'The feasts of the LORD, which you shall proclaim to be holy convocations, these are My feasts."**

Notice, the word *feasts* is plural.

Leviticus 23:3:

> 'Six days shall work be done, but the seventh
> day is a Sabbath of solemn rest, a holy convocation.
> You shall do no work on it; it is the Sabbath of the
> Lord in all your dwellings.

Please keep in mind that the above verses refer to the Saturday Sabbath, the weekly Sabbath. It is called a day of rest, a holy convocation.

Leviticus 23:4-7:

> 'These are the feasts of the Lord, holy convocations
> [we could say Sabbaths] **which you shall proclaim at their
> appointed times.**
>> '**On the fourteenth day of the first month at twilight
>> is the Lord's Passover.**
>> '**And on the fifteenth day of the same month is the
>> Feast of Unleavened Bread to the Lord; seven days you must
>> eat unleavened bread.**
>> '**On the first day you shall have a holy convocation;
>> you shall do no customary work on it.'"**

Now God is talking now about the preparation day of the Passover, or the first day of Passover, and He refers to it as a holy convocation or Sabbath.

The Passover was an Old Testament type of Jesus Christ. Jesus is the Passover Lamb of the New Testament. He is our substitute. That is what the Passover Lamb was to the children of Israel — their substitute.

When the children of Israel were in bondage in Egypt, the Pharaoh would not let them depart even though Moses brought him the edict from God. God firmly said, "I will permit the death angel to come to the house of Egypt as a sign of my wrath and judgment upon Egypt; every firstborn child of every household will die because of Pharaoh's hardness of heart."

However, in the houses of Goshen where the children of Israel resided, God said, "Take a lamb, a male lamb of the first year, without a spot, without a wrinkle, without a blemish in it, and kill it." They were instructed to take the blood from that lamb and paint it on the two side posts and on the upper doorpost of their houses. The Lamb's body was to be split open, roasted with fire and stretched out full-length both ways. God said they were to follow His directions so that when the angel of death got to each individual house, he would see the blood and pass over that house, and no firstborn in that house would die.

The death angel "passed over" the children of Israel — that is where the term *Passover* originated. But what saved the people? It was the blood of the sacrificial lamb. What did John the Baptist say at the banks of the River Jordan when he looked up and saw Jesus? **"Behold! The lamb of God who takes away the sin of the world"** (John 1:29). Jesus is the Passover Lamb; His shed blood has saved us.

God instructed the children of Israel to prepare the Passover lamb on the 14th day of Nisan. Likewise, I submit to you that the 14th day of Nisan is the very same day of the year on which the Lord Jesus Christ died.

Jesus' Death Fulfilled the Passover

The death of Jesus was to fulfill the Passover. In the year in which Jesus died, the 14th day of Nisan (when the lamb was supposed to be slain) was on a Wednesday, not a Friday.

Now let us count: At sundown, at the end of the day (the Hebrew day ended at 6 p.m. when night began) the Bible said they took His body down from the cross. They could not allow bodies to remain on the cross during that particular holy convocation or Sabbath. Why? Because it was the Passover.

That was on a Wednesday night. Wednesday night was the first night in the grave, and Thursday the first day. Thursday night was the second night in the grave, and Friday was the second day. Friday night was the third night in the grave, and Saturday was the third day. When the women came to the tomb, they had to wait for the weekly Sabbath to pass. The end of the Sabbath, technically, would be 6 a.m. Sunday morning. The Bible says that when the women came, it was not yet Sunday morning.

Matthew 28:1:

Now after the Sabbath, as the first day of the week began to dawn, Mary Magdalene and the other Mary came to see the tomb.

They said among themselves, "Who is going to remove the stone?" When they came to the tomb, the stone was already rolled away. The tomb was empty and an angel of the Lord was sitting on the stone. The angel said, "What are you doing here looking for the living among the dead? He is not dead, but alive as He said, and He will appear before you in Galilee."

Jesus was already risen when they came, "... as the first day of the week began to dawn." Actually, Jesus rose from the dead somewhere between sundown Saturday and sunrise Sunday.

Thus, there is no such thing, biblically, as "Good Friday." Jesus did not die on Friday; He died on Wednesday, the 14th day of Nisan. He perfectly and accurately fulfilled the shadow and type, according to the Old Testament, of the Passover Lamb. When Jesus was resurrected from the dead, He rose triumphant over death, hell and the grave!

Do you think that the punishment for our sin was for someone to simply die on the cross? If that were so, then the two thieves crucified with Jesus could have paid the price. But they could not because the real punishment was to go into Hell itself and serve our time, separated from God.

Jesus was the only one who could do that, and He did that on our behalf. After divine justice was satisfied, God said, "It is enough!" Jesus rose from the dead and ascended to heaven.

He is there now, alive and well and seated at the right hand of the Father! Praise God, we serve a *risen* Savior!

Nugget No.13
What If Jesus Were Black?

"Joy to the world, the Lord is come...." That is a phrase of a song we often hear during the Christmas season. Songs of adoration and praise to our Savior and Lord Jesus Christ flow from the lips of millions of men, women and children throughout the world. For Christians, Christmas is one of the most important times of the year, as the birth of our King of kings is celebrated. And for millions who do not know Him, Christmas is still considered the highlight of the year.

There is always a special air of excitement and joy as the Christmas holiday season approaches, bringing with it a sense of love and a show of affection that we really find no other time of year. There is the gift-giving, family togetherness, friendships renewed, old hurts forgiven, wounds healed, and of course, food, food, food!

Despite it all, however, most of the folks involved in all the hoopla do not even realize why they are doing all this celebrating!

They do not know that Jesus Christ is the real reason for the season.

Commercialism —
Borne on the Back of Our Redeemer

People get in a frenzy, an almost compulsive buying, giving mode. They go crazy making bills that they cannot afford to pay off for two years down the line! That is commercialism — borne on the back of our Redeemer — and it has absolutely nothing to do with the birth and true celebration of our Savior and Lord Jesus Christ. It is just a way man has capitalized on the birth of Jesus to put money into his own pockets. And the commercialism grows worse each year.

I love Christmas, so don't get me wrong. My family and I have a great time. And I love buying presents for them. Unfortunately, however, too many Christians have lost sight of the reason for the season. They, along with the un-Believers, have gotten wrapped up in the commercialism and buying syndrome.

Despite all the craziness that goes along with the Christmas season, I can see some elements of good. For example, the Christmas season is the only time many people ever think about giving anybody anything! It's the only time of the year that a lot of folk express any joy, or exhibit any affection or love toward family or friends. Plus, it's the only time some people ever set foot in a church, besides on Mother's Day and Easter (or Resurrection Day). So, there are some positive things.

The celebration of Christmas brings with it some good things, and some great traditions, as well as some odd conceptions. For example, although Christmas is a time to celebrate the birth of

Jesus, some people have not yet realized that Jesus grew up. He is no longer in the manger, and He is no longer a child. And He now, forever, makes intercession for us at the right hand of the Father God.

When the season is over, some of those odd conceptions linger on for a lifetime. Many Christians still prefer to see Jesus through their own eyes and traditions, rather than for whom He truly was and is. Way past the Christmas season, you can hear them praise His name and say "Hallelujah" to the mighty King. Yet the only King they envision is the one they have seen in paintings and drawings on thousands of walls the world over. You know the photographs I am referring to: The namby-pamby, frail, effeminate-looking Jesus, barefoot, pale and very European. At Christmas and beyond, this is the figure of Jesus that has been etched in the minds of millions.

God's People — Swallowing Man's Lies

I find it interesting to see how easily God's people — not just sinners — but God's people follow the crowd and swallow the lies that man has created and perpetuated throughout the years. God's people are supposed to study, so they can more readily discern the truth from a lie. But if a person hears something long enough — whether it is a truth or a lie — he will begin to believe, repeat, and eventually act upon it.

You can see why the Christmas season has become such a commercial success. It is because too few people have been guarding their eyes and ears. They have fallen for the sales pitches, gone out, and bought just about everything they could walk out of the stores with! They buy, buy, buy, and when it is all over, they cry, cry, cry, because they have to pay all those bills they made! Unfortunately, the commercialism of Christmas continues to work!

In the same way they have fallen for the salesman's pitch, people have bought the idea that the real Jesus is who they see in those paintings and drawings, simply because that is what they have always seen. There is absolutely no way you could tell some people that Jesus really did not look like that — even though a study of Scripture will help even a half-way intelligent person understand some things about the way Jesus looked in the flesh.

What if I told you Jesus just might not look like that guy hanging in the frame on your wall? Suppose — just suppose — the Man you have been calling your Savior and Lord had skin a little darker than what you have always believed? Suppose He had slanted eyes and black hair? Or, suppose the Jesus whom you believe healed the sick and raised the dead — the Jesus who redeemed you and saved you from the pit of hell — was black in skin color? Would it matter to you? Would it be cause for you to reject Christianity altogether?

Would Jesus Lose His Credibility If He Were Black?

Mind you, Jesus would still have done all you say you believe He did for you. He still would be the Son of God. He still would have gone to hell and defeated the devil, and He would still have shed His blood and given His life that you might live. He still would be the same Jesus who rose from the dead and is now seated at the right hand of the Father God. Even though He would still be the same, would you — could you be the same devoted Believer in Christ if He were Black?

114

I know a lot of you will get upset reading what I just said. But it's on you to check yourself and find out why you feel so upset, if you are.

If you discovered that Jesus' skin were black, could you still sing "I Love You Lord" or "I Want to Be Like Jesus"? When you or your children sing "Away in a Manger" and "Silent Night," in your wildest imagination, could you picture a Black Jesus being the One you are worshipping and singing about? If not, why not? I have never seen Jesus and neither have you, so it is just as possible for Him to have been dark-Black, Asian, or Indian as it is for you to only imagine Him as fair-skinned and White.

I find it interesting that so many people find it hard to even imagine Jesus being Black, yet they so easily accept that Jesus is White? Why? And why should it matter?

I am not trying to be funny. But I believe the question I have posed is something you might want to think about. Not because what you think makes any difference in whom Jesus is and what He did, but because it could make a difference in you and who you say you are. And if ever there were a time we, as Christians, needed to examine ourselves about this matter and other issues, the time is now.

This issue of skin color has been a plaguing problem in America more than anywhere else in the world, dating back to the time of slavery. And the problem exists and prevails, even in the midst of the joy of the Christmas season. All of the race bias is based on ignorance, runaway insecurities, and inferiority complexes that Satan has used to divide not only sinners, but also God's people. It is a blotch on the Body of Christ. It is not Christ-like! It is not of God!

You can take what I say with a grain of salt. But I hope you will at least think about it as you celebrate Jesus this Christmas.

You can consider what I have said simply as food for thought at a very joyous time of year — a time for joy and a time for examining yourself and your Christian walk.

With all said and done, nothing changes the fact that Jesus remains who He is — King of kings, Lord of lords — no matter what anybody thinks. Keep that in mind, and when Christmas comes and goes, you should still be able to say that you want to be like Jesus, and still be able to proudly sing, "Joy to the world, the Lord is come...."

Nugget No.14

A Message to Ministers

Being a minister of the Gospel is the highest calling one could ever have in life. It is the highest honor, privilege and the greatest opportunity that anyone can have to make an impact upon mankind and the world in general. As a minister of the Gospel, you are an advocate for the heavenly Father. Ministering His Word is your vocation. It is not just an average kind of profession that you are in. You are an advocate for the things of God! Isn't that a wonderful privilege! Think about that and then you will begin to realize just how blessed you really are.

Some occupations are designed to take care of the physical body. Others cater to the soul. Some professions simply titillate the flesh. Being an athlete is great. Being a doctor is wonderful. Being president of the United States is a marvelous achievement. But no job is better than the one ministers have been called to: serving mankind in a way that can help transform them from the inside out through the Word of God. To be able to influence men and women at their very core is not only honorable, fulfilling, and special, but it is humbling.

I encourage you not to take your calling lightly. Stay wise to the enemy's tactics by staying wise to God's Word. Know that the enemy is ever lurking, ready to steal, kill, and destroy not only your witness and your work on behalf of the Kingdom of God, but your very life. But greater is He who is in you than he who is in the world! Hallelujah!

Whatever knowledge of God's Word you have gained, use it. The ball is in your court. Be ready to put into action all those things you have learned during your study of God's Word, and your own personal prayer time. Continue to study diligently and to pray fervently.

Take inventory of your personal life. If there is anything that you need to get right with God, do it quickly. If your personal lifestyle is not right, your ministry will be a mess. Do not allow a tacky lifestyle to hinder your progress in the work of the Kingdom. There is no need to walk around saying you are "on top and rising," when you know you need to get some things in order. Get things right. Get rid of all your baggage and then you will be able to freely move in the spirit and out into your ministry.

Pursue with vigor the visions and dreams God has placed inside you. God does not need you half-stepping. Give it your all! As you do that, moving in faith and love to do the will of the Father, you will experience the Word working in your life.

Do not be concerned about the circumstances, nor about what someone else is doing, or how well they may be progressing. Keep your eyes on what the Lord called you to do, moving in step with, in line with, and on time with God. Keep your eyes on the Word, and act on it. You will not go wrong if you do that.

I exhort you and encourage you to fight the good fight of faith as you move out into your ministry!

For a complete list of books and tapes by Dr. Frederick K.C. Price, or to receive his publication, *Ever Increasing Faith Messenger,* write

Dr. Fred Price
Crenshaw Christian Center
P.O. Box 90000
Los Angeles CA 90009

BOOKS BY FREDERICK K.C. PRICE, PH.D.

HIGH FINANCE
(God Financial Plan: Tithes and Offerings)

HOW FAITH WORKS

IS HEALING FOR ALL?

HOW TO OBTAIN STRONG FAITH
Six Principles

NOW FAITH IS

THE HOLY SPIRIT —
The Missing Ingredient

FAITH, FOOLISHNESS, OR PRESUMPTION?

THANK GOD FOR EVERYTHING?

HOW TO BELIEVE GOD FOR A MATE

LIVING IN THE REALM OF THE SPIRIT

THE ORIGIN OF SATAN

CONCERNING THEM WHICH ARE ASLEEP

HOMOSEXUALITY:
State of Birth or State of Mind?

PROSPERITY ON GOD'S TERMS

WALKING IN GOD'S WORD
Through His Promises

KEYS TO SUCCESSFUL MINISTRY

NAME IT AND CLAIM IT!
The Power of Positive Confession

THE VICTORIOUS, OVERCOMING LIFE
(A Verse-by-Verse Study on the Book of Colossians)

A NEW LAW FOR A NEW PEOPLE

THE PROMISED LAND
(A New Era for the Body of Christ)

THREE KEYS TO POSITIVE CONFESSION

THE WAY, THE WALK,
AND THE WARFARE OF THE BELIEVER
(A Verse-by-Verse Study on the Book of Ephesians)

BEWARE! THE LIES OF SATAN

TESTING THE SPIRITS

THE CHASTENING OF THE LORD

IDENTIFIED WITH CHRIST:
A Complete Cycle From Defeat to Victory

THE CHRISTIAN FAMILY:
Practical Insight for Family Living
(formerly MARRIAGE AND THE FAMILY)

THE HOLY SPIRIT:
THE HELPER WE ALL NEED

FIVE LITTLE FOXES OF FAITH

BUILDING ON A FIRM FOUNDATION

DR. PRICE'S GOLDEN NUGGETS
A Treasury of Wisdom for Both Ministers and Laypeople

About the Author

Frederick K. C. Price, Ph.D., founded Crenshaw Christian Center in Los Angeles, California, in 1973, with a congregation of some 300 people. Today, the church's membership numbers well over 18,000 members of various ethnic backgrounds.

Crenshaw Christian Center, home of the renowned 10,146-seat FaithDome, has a staff of more than 300 employees. Included on its 30-acre grounds are a Ministry Training Institute, the Frederick K.C. Price III elementary and junior and senior high schools, as well as the FKCP III Preschool.

The *Ever Increasing Faith* television and radio broadcasts are outreaches of Crenshaw Christian Center. The television program is viewed on more than 100 stations worldwide. The radio program airs on more than 40 stations across the country and internationally.

Dr. Price travels extensively, teaching on the Word of Faith simply and understandably in the power of the Holy Spirit. He is the author of several books on faith, divine healing, prosperity, and the Holy Spirit.

In 1990, Dr. Price founded the Fellowship of Inner-City Word of Faith Ministries (FICWFM) for the purpose of fostering and spreading the faith message among independent ministries located in the metropolitan areas of the United States.

Notes

Notes

Notes

Notes

Notes

Notes

Notes

Notes

Notes